chancellorsville 1863

jackson's lightning strike

CARL SMITH

chancellorsville 1863

jackson's lightning strike

Praeger Illustrated Military History Series

Westport, Connecticut
London

Library of Congress Cataloging-in-Publication Data

Smith, Carl, 1946-
　　Chancellorsville 1863: Jackson's lightning strike / Carl Smith.
　　　　p. cm. – (Praeger illustrated military history, ISSN 1547-206X)
　　Originally published: Oxford: Osprey, 1998.
　　Includes bibliographical references and index.
　　ISBN 0-275-98445-1 (alk. paper)
　　1. Chancellorsville, Battle of, Chancellorsville, Va., 1863. I. Title. II. Series.
　　E475.35.S65　　2004
　　973.7'34–dc22　　2004050376

British Library Cataloguing in Publication Data is available.

First published in paperback in 1998 by Osprey Publishing Limited, Elms Court,
Chapel Way, Botley, Oxford OX2 9LP. All rights reserved.

Copyright © 2004 by Osprey Publishing Limited

Library of Congress Catalog Card Number: 2004050376
ISBN: 0-275-98445-1
ISSN: 1547-206X

Praeger Publishers, 88 Post Road West, Westport, CT 06881
An imprint of Greenwood Publishing Group, Inc.
www.praeger.com

Printed in China through World Print Ltd.

The paper used in this book complies with the Permanent Paper Standard issued
by the National Information Standards Organization (Z39.48-1984).

10　9　8　7　6　5　4　3　2　1

ILLUSTRATED BY: **Adam Hook**

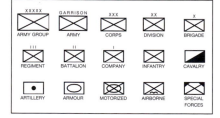
CONTENTS

ORIGINS OF THE CAMPAIGN

Chancellorsville, a lone farmhouse situated at the junction of two roads a few miles west of Fredericksburg, lies 50 miles north of Richmond and 25 miles east of Culpeper, south of the Rappahannock River and near the eastern edge of the Spotsylvania Wilderness. This area has been so-called from the earliest times because of its thick collection of oak, pine, maple, and dogwood trees interspersed with springy underbrush and dense thickets covering the gently rolling hills of central Northern Virginia. Much of the old growth was cut down to fuel a colonial mine and has been replaced by hardy secondary growth scrub oak and pine thickets. Even today dense brush makes walking the Spotsylvania Wilderness difficult.

The battle of Chancellorsville could more aptly be called the second battle of Fredericksburg because the battle which General Ambrose Burnside started in the frigid December of 1862 involved an inconclusive river crossing and a sound defeat for his assaulting troops. However, Lee did not complete his victory by counter-attacking across the river and driving the Federals off the east bank. The Army of the Potomac loomed dark and foreboding on the winter landscape across the Rappahannock from the nearly destroyed town. An unofficial truce developed in the harsh winter of 1862-63: it was too cold for the Southerners to attack; the Army of the Potomac was too demoralized to launch an offensive; and the ground was too frozen to dig graves. Both sides waited uneasily for spring.

With spring the waiting would end, for Robert E. Lee knew that the South was losing this war of attrition. For the South to win, it had to fight a fast and aggressive war, and not stagnate in fortified camps. Events now in motion would forever change the war.

On the last day of April and during the first week of May 1863, Robert E. Lee and Stonewall Jackson fought off Joseph Hooker's well planned major offensive, driving off his superior force and again denying Union troops egress to Richmond. What started as Hooker's master stroke became Jackson's and Lee's last great victory. When the Chancellorsville campaign ended, the Union had lost over 17,000 troops and the Confederates, 13,000. The Union Army had been defeated soundly and the door to a northern invasion by the Army of Northern Virginia was open. However, the face of warfare, strategy, and ultimately the Civil War, irrevocably changed with Stonewall Jackson's death.

CHRONOLOGY

December 1862 was brutally cold, and Burnside's attempted mid-December crossing of the Rappahannock to attack Fredericksburg failed miserably with the terrain, entrenched Confederates, and winter working against him. The Army of the Potomac's morale plummeted and Burnside effected winter quarters almost across the river from Fredericksburg; each day there, Union pickets could see pickets of the army which had stymied their advance and run them back across the icy waters. When Burnside hinted to his Grand Division commanders in early 1863 that he intended another attack in almost exactly the same fashion, they feared great losses. Two went directly to Lincoln without Burnside's knowledge or consent, pleading that the army was not unwilling to fight, but that another costly assault might not only fail in its objective, but might leave Washington and

Ambrose Everett Burnside was a genial man, chosen to command because other candidates were too political or too controversial. He had designed a carbine, and although only a moderately good soldier, he was a welcome change after McClellan.

LEFT Woods surrounding Chancellorsville were filled with secondary growth that was thick and tough, and made concentrated military maneuvers difficult. The primary growth had been cut for fuel nearly 100 years earlier.

This view of the 150th Pennsylvania gives a small idea of the Union encampment which the Southerners saw across the Rappahannock from Fredericksburg in the winter of 1862 and spring of 1863.

the entire north open to attack if Lee chose to press his advantage. When Burnside next asked to be relieved of command of the Army of the Potomac, Lincoln listened.

Lincoln replaced Burnside with Hooker. Although General Joseph Hooker had not been among the generals who had gone to Washington, he had a record of openly criticizing his superiors. In fact, because of this behavior during the Mexican-American War, General Winfield Scott had denied Hooker a commission when the Civil War started. With the support of friends, Hooker went to see Lincoln after First Manassas and commented that he was a better commander than those on the field that day. Although aware of Hooker's boastfulness and habit of criticizing superiors, Lincoln was impressed with his self-assurance and gave him a commission. But Henry Halleck, who succeeded Scott, was concerned about Hooker's ability to turn his boast into reality.

Hooker's nickname ("Fighting Joe Hooker") had come about as a result of a miscommunication earlier in the war. A reporter had asked Hooker what he was doing, and he had replied, "Fighting." The reporter had quoted him, saying, "Fighting – Joe Hooker." A telegrapher had missent it as "Fightin' Joe Hooker." When newspaper reporters nationwide quoted his response, a moniker was born.

Hooker was not known as a loyal subordinate, and when Lincoln replaced Burnside, he warned Hooker that he wanted an officer who would fight and who would "use all his troops." The President told Hooker that he had two jobs: to defeat Lee's Army of Northern Virginia, and to protect Washington, D.C. Lincoln should have guessed that Hooker was a poor choice when almost immediately upon his appointment Hooker began talking about marching on Richmond.

As Lee was a moving target and Richmond was stationary, Hooker felt that if Richmond fell, the Confederates would be demoralized and the war would end. This was sound theory, but would prove difficult to achieve as long as the Army of Northern Virginia was free to act. Lee's army was filled with crack soldiers. Civilians residing in Richmond would worry about Hooker's close proximity and would demand Confederate troops to protect their homes and businesses. In so doing they would act as unwitting allies to the North by pressuring Southern

General Thomas Meagher, commander of the famous Irish Brigade, which was nearly decimated following Burnside's orders at Fredericksburg, commanded the remnants of the brigade in the Chancellorsville campaign.

Appointed by Lincoln despite his boastful nature and constant comments denigrating his superiors, General Hooker was a good subordinate commander. He reorganized the cavalry into a corps and restructured the Army of the Potomac.

leaders to capitulate if the capitol was threatened. However, if Hooker was to defeat Lee he had first to overcome severe internal military problems.

In January 1863 the Army of the Potomac was not an effective fighting force. Morale was at an all-time low, Lee had soundly defeated them, Jackson had run circles around Pope and had burned a Federal supply depot at Second Manassas. The Army of the Potomac was camped opposite the site of one of the Union's worst defeats. Burnside's near-suicidal attack on Fredericksburg had shattered the Irish Brigade in a futile assault across a river and up a steep slope to attack a well-defended hill where the Confederates were entrenched. Where to find the Confederates was not Hooker's problem; how to defeat them was. A direct assault was out – Burnside had tried and failed. A more sophisticated multi-pronged attack with simultaneous threats to Richmond, Lee's troops, and Fredericksburg might confuse Lee and let Hooker bring his entire army into play.

Hooker was a good organizer. One of his first actions was to restructure the Army of the Potomac from Burnside's cumbersome Grand Division structure into the corps structure it would retain throughout the Civil War. Most importantly, he formed the cavalry into a corps under Stoneman by removing it from the tender mercies of division and corps commanders who until then had used the penny-packeted cavalry ineffectively. Then he assigned corps insignia to distinguish and identify soldiers. Morale of his 120,000 troops was rock bottom when Hooker assumed command, but within weeks he improved rations, increased supplies, saw that men were sheltered, enforced sanitary regulations, instituted a series of leaves and furloughs, and with regular drills began to instil an *esprit de corps* in his men. Desertions and absences without leave plummeted, and morale improved. The army began to feel and act like an army again.

Finally Hooker formed the Bureau of Military Information, under Col. Sharpe. Until then the Pinkertons had loosely managed a network of spies and intelligence gathering, but their information had proved notoriously inaccurate. Using military men to gather, sift, evaluate, and report information to a single source, Hooker would have a more accurate and clearly defined picture of Confederate troop movements and strength than any previous Union commander.

After being relieved of command of the Army of the Potomac, Burnside was appointed commander of the Department of the Ohio, a position which kept him from having to command too many troops on campaign.

Next Hooker began to formulate his plan of attack, and the newly instituted cavalry corps was instrumental to its success. Secrecy was paramount, and Hooker held information on the upcoming campaign on a "need to know" basis, keeping even corps commanders in the dark so there could be no possible leaks to the enemy. He wanted to create threats on all sides of the Army of Northern Virginia and then strike at Lee's weakest point when he moved elsewhere to counter a threat. It was a sound plan.

The build-up to Chancellorsville

13 December – At Fredericksburg, Ambrose Burnside attacks across the Rappahannock in a wintery crossing. Meade's and Gibbon's men cause Jackson's lines to crumble, but Longstreet on Marye's (pronounced Marie's) Heights soundly defeats Hooker and Sumner when their divisions cross. The attack is an abysmal failure, and at the end, the Federals still have the tenuous hold on the city with which they started, and the Confederates still command the heights above. A Federal officer says, "It was a great slaughter..." and Lee commented, "I wish these people would go away and leave us alone." The Federals suffer 12,653 casualties; the Confederates, 5,309.

14 December – Burnside orders the attack renewed but Hooker, Sumner, and Franklin dissuade him. Lee does not counter-attack, but looms on the heights over the Union Army. With this untenable situation, Burnside orders the Army of the Potomac to withdraw from Fredericksburg to the east bank of the Rappahannock.

22 December – Burnside meets with Lincoln. Controversy over just who is responsible for the debacle includes everyone from the president down to division commanders.

29 December – At Chickasaw Bayou, near Vicksburg, Sherman takes heavy losses, and his action is compared to the Fredericksburg defeat.

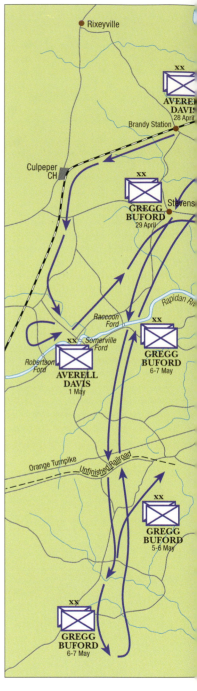

ABOVE **Although nearly a third of Lee's men went south and east with Longstreet, the majority of his army was encamped in winter quarters at Fredericksburg. The countryside around Fredericksburg had been fought over and foraging was poor. As a third element of Hooker's plan to confound Lee, Stoneman's cavalry corps was to**

EASTERN THEATER, VIRGINIA. STONEMAN'S RAID, APRIL 1863

swing wide, going first north, then west, and finally south to harass Lee and cut communications and supply lines. All this was supposed to occur while Sedgwick threatened Fredericksburg from the south and east and while Hooker slipped the remainder of his army across the Rappahannock and converged on Chancellorsville.

30 December – Burnside plans another assault, but when word reaches Lincoln, he tells Burnside, "You must not make a general movement of the army without letting me know."

31 December 1862 – Burnside goes to Washington to testify in a court martial. Lincoln admits loyal West Virginia to the Union as the 35th state.

1 January 1863 – Lincoln signs the Emancipation Proclamation, which declares, "...all persons held as slaves within said designated States, and parts of States, are, and henceforward shall be free." The proclamation states that slaves in areas of the South not under Union control will be freed as soon as the Union

Although commanding a new cavalry corps, General Stoneman (central figure with arms crossed) and his staff were not sure how to wield the weapon Hooker had forged for them. His slowness and his inability to reach his destination contributed to Hooker's defeat at Chancellorsville.

occupies them. In an open letter, Burnside plans to resign for "the public good" but Lincoln persuades him to stay.

5 January – Burnside again proposes to Lincoln an assault on Fredericksburg, and as leverage, includes his resignation.

7 January – General Halleck backs Burnside, but reminds him the objective is "... not Richmond, but the defeat... of Lee's army."

8 January – Lincoln writes Burnside, "I do not yet see... changing the command of the A.P.... I should not wish... the resignation of your command."

19 January – The Army of the Potomac begins its second attempt to cross the river and take Fredericksburg.

20 January – Winter rains turn the red Virginia clay to a sticky, slimy mud. As a result, Burnside writes, "... We felt the winter campaign had ended."

21 January – A fierce winter storm slashes the entire east coast, and Burnside's assault slows to a snail's pace.

22 January – Winter rains continue, causing the river to rise, and this ends the Fredericksburg Campaign. Burnside's task becomes not how to advance on Fredericksburg, but how to return along nearly impassable roads to his winter camp.

23 January – Burnside issues orders to remove Hooker, Franklin, and Smith from command. He sends Lincoln a request for a meeting to discuss their insubordination and the low morale of his officer corps and troops.

25 January – Lincoln relieves Burnside, Smith and Franklin. He appoints Hooker commander of the Army of the Potomac.

26 January – As Hooker assumes command, Lincoln writes, "I believe you to be a brave and skillful soldier... you do not mix politics with your profession. You have confidence..." Then he admonishes Hooker, "During Gen. Burnside's command of the Army, you... thwarted him as much as you could. I have heard... of your recently saying that both the Army and the Government needed a Dictator." Lincoln notes, "It was not for this, but rather in spite of it, that I have given you the command. Only those generals who gain successes can set up dictators. What I now ask of you is military success, and I will risk the dictatorship."

5 February – Hooker abolishes the Grand Divisions of the Army of the

ABOVE **Stoneman reached Kelly's Ford on the Rappahannock on 21 April 1863. Poor weather and timidity kept his raid from producing more than a few burned railroad bridges, and the Union cavalry was ineffective in the Chancellorsville campaign.**

The net result of Stoneman's raid, other than showing that Union cavalry could act as a unit, was a few destroyed railroad bridges. Many were repaired and functioning again within a few days of Stoneman's passage.

Potomac. He assigns new corps commanders, including General Stoneman, to lead the new cavalry corps and begins reconnaissance of Lee's position.

18 February – Lee sends two of Longstreet's divisions east to forage and to defend from possible attack up the James or the Peninsula.

23 February – Jeb Stuart's cavalry harasses Union cavalry outposts, and Union commanders want a counter-attack by Union cavalry to put the Confederate cavalry on the defensive.

3 March – Lincoln signs the first Federal draft law. All male citizens between twenty and forty-five, except for the mentally unfit, felons, those with specific categories of dependents, and specific state and government officials, are eligible for the draft. However, a drafted man could pay $300 to another man to serve in his place.

6 March – Stoneman's cavalry re-arms with Sharps breech-loading carbines which gives them increased firepower.

16 March – Union cavalry commander Gen. Wm. Averell presents Stoneman with his plan to raid Southern cavalry commander Fitz Lee's positions at Culpeper, VA, and thus let the South know that its cavalry superiority is no longer uncontested.

17 March – Averell's 800 men attack Lee's 2,000 men, taking them by surprise, but Stuart arrives unexpectedly. When he hears this, Averell withdraws, not realizing that Stuart is alone except for his staff and doesn't

lead reinforcements. Hooker berates Averell for his show of bravado.

25 March – General Burnside is appointed commander of the Department of the Ohio.

30 March – A skirmish occurs at Zoan Church, Va, between Federal and Confederate forces.

2 April – A "bread riot" occurs in Richmond, Va, and Confederate President Jefferson Davis calls out police and militia to dispel the rioters.

6 April – Lincoln meets with General Hooker, telling him, "Our prime objective is the enemies' army... not... Richmond."

12 April – To Lincoln, Hooker proposes a flanking action to turn Lee's left and put Union cavalry between Lee and Richmond.

15 April – Lincoln tells Hooker he is concerned about Stoneman's slow progress on the Rappahannock.

27 April – Hooker moves troops up the Rappahannock near the fords over the river, beginning his advance on Lee's position at Fredericksburg and initiating the Campaign for Chancellorsville.

28 April – The Army of the Potomac begins crossing the Rappahannock in an area called the Wilderness. Seeing the beginnings of a flanking movement, townspeople in Fredericksburg ring the Episcopal Church bell as a warning.

This is Fredericksburg in around late 1862 or early January 1863. Note the misty fog over the city, where the weather is frigid despite the lack of snow on the ground. The heights behind the city are barely visible.

29 April – Crossing at Kelly's and U.S. fords, the Army of the Potomac positions itself on the left flank of Lee's army. Sedgwick's action at White Oak Run (Fitzhugh's Crossing) south of Fredericksburg creates a diversion for the greater Federal crossing at the northern fords.

30 April – Hooker sets up camp around the Chancellor farmhouse, grandiosely named Chancellorsville. Stoneman reaches Raccoon Ford. Hooker tells his men, "The last three days have determined that our enemy must ingloriously fly, or come out from behind their defense and give us battle on our ground, where certain destruction awaits." In Fredericksburg Lee evaluates the unprecedented actions and tries to determine where the real threat lies: with Stoneman; to the left flank with Hooker; to Fredericksburg with Sedgwick; or to the south at White Oak Run (where Federal troops had feinted and then moved toward Fredericksburg). The die was cast.

Lee had grown accustomed to McClellan's inaction and to Burnside's ineptitude, however, Hooker's decisive move against him posed a real threat. Hooker's attack was well-conceived and presented danger on several fronts. Briefly Lee regretted sending Longstreet south and east, but then he got down to the business of stopping Hooker!

OPPOSING COMMANDERS

CONFEDERATE COMMANDERS

Robert E. Lee

Robert E. Lee is probably the most revered commander of either side. The fifth son of Revolutionary War hero Light Horse Harry Lee, he attended West Point and served as an officer of engineers prior to the Mexican-American War. His active career began with the Mexican-American War, and thereafter he was in charge of West Point and commanded the marines which stormed John Brown's position at Harper's Ferry to capture the abolitionist. When offered command of the Union Army, he turned it down and resigned from Federal service because he would not fight against Virginia, which had seceded from the Union. Related by marriage to George Washington, he was a plantation owner without many slaves, and he freed those willed to him by his father-in-law. He was a humanitarian, but a Virginian first and foremost.

An aggressive commander who knew that boldness and calculated risk could often throw an opponent off guard, Lee was a career soldier. He was not the original Southern commander, but soon gained attention for his astute military skill and his bold action. Following Joe Johnston's wounding, he became commander of the Army of Northern Virginia.

Recognizing Stonewall Jackson's aggressive nature, Lee soon formed a fondness for the ex-Virginia Military Institute (VMI) teacher, and together they turned the Army of Northern Virginia into a feared fighting machine, trouncing the Union in the Peninsula, up and down the Shenandoah Valley, at Second Manassas, Fredericksburg, and Chancellorsville.

After Jackson's death, Lee never found another commander as astute and aggressive; with the loss of the South's "right arm," as he termed Jackson, he seemed to lose his edge. At Gettysburg Lee's hopes for an independent South were to lie crushed, ending at Appomattox after two more years of fierce fighting.

Lee was a canny general who never recklessly risked his men or resources but who was unafraid to undertake a calculated risk, because he knew that to win a great prize, a man had to take great chances. After the war, Lee went on to become president of what is now Washington and Lee University. He died in 1870.

Stonewall Jackson

Thomas Jonathan Jackson graduated from West Point in 1846 and served in the Mexican-American War as an artillery officer. In 1852 he became an artillery instructor at VMI. When the war came, he was a colonel of Virginia militia, and he served at Harper's Ferry until J.E. Johnston superseded him. At First Manassas, General Bernard Bee rallied his South Carolinians saying, "Rally behind the Virginians. There stands Jackson like a stone wall." The nickname stuck, and he became Stonewall Jackson.

Jackson demanded great things of his troops, and they performed to his expectations. He maintained tight secrecy about orders, often directing his commanders from the front, sending them from one crossroads to the next so no one would be aware of his true destination. This gave him a military advantage in a time when spying was simply hanging around soldiers and keeping your ears

This photo of Robert E. Lee was taken in 1863, probably around the time of Chancellorsville, when he was in top condition (and before the many cares of the later war years wore him down).

Jackson was healthy and confident in this 1862 photo: he did not exhibit the thin features of the hard campaigner evident in his last picture. Note the apparent absence of braid on his coat cuffs.

open. His men routinely marched so long and fast that they were known as "Jackson's Foot Cavalry." In the Shenandoah Valley he defeated three Union armies and kept the valley safe within the Confederacy. At one point he defeated Fremont on 8 June 1862 at Cross Keys and then Shields at Port Republic on 9 June. His performance during the Seven Days Battles was lackluster, and it appears that he was at his best when exercising an independent command.

Jackson was a man of many idiosyncrasies, who cared little for fancy uniforms and wore his battered VMI kepi until weeks before his death. Some of his men called him "Old Blue Light", from the way his piercing blue eyes glowed at the prospect of combat. He often stood with his arm held above his head, which he felt improved his circulation, and he always stood while reading, claiming that his stance put his organs in their natural position. He would stick his head into a bucket of cold water with his eyes open to improve his eyesight, and he had a fondness for lemons. He was a staunch Presbyterian, and somewhat stand-offish, but he never demanded from his men that which he was unwilling to give himself, and they respected him. A fiercely proud commander, Jackson tolerated no deviation from his orders. He had A.P. Hill (with whom he was friendly) relieved of command and put under arrest for an infraction of orders. Hill never forgave him.

Jackson had an uncanny knack for moving his troops quickly and then putting them in exactly the right place at the right time to aid the Confederacy. Together with Robert E. Lee, he formed half of the South's dynamic fighting team, the two men seeming to read the other's mind and then act accordingly, to produce the best possible military result.

Jackson defeated Pope at Second Manassas. He was given command of the II Corps, Army of Northern Virginia. Justifiably, his most famous feat was the audacious march across the front of the Union Army at Chancellorsville, flanking them and routing XI Corps. They thought he was retreating until his troops charged the poorly protected Union right flank and slammed into the XI Corps, sending its bewildered troops reeling.

He was wounded on 2 May 1863 by nervous Southern pickets while beyond Confederate lines studying Union positions. His left arm was successfully amputated, but pneumonia set in and he died on 10 May 1863. Lee said of Jackson's death, "I have lost my right arm."

Jackson was a general with insight and an almost uncanny ability to detect an enemy's weak spot and then position his troops to spearhead an attack against that area, regardless of how difficult it was or how long it took to arrive at the point. His loss was a great blow to the South psychologically, as well as removing from them a commander who rarely lost a battle and intimidated the enemy. His final words were, "Let us cross over the river and rest under the shade of the trees."

Jubal Early

Jubal Early was a West Point graduate of 1837 who fought the Seminoles and then resigned to practice law. He was elected to the house of delegates and then commanded Virginia volunteers in the Mexican-American War. Although he voted against secession, like Lee he was a Virginian, and he promptly entered service of the new government when Virginia left the Union.

Early fought in all the major engagements with the Army of Northern Virginia from 1862 through 1864. He was a good commander, but hit his stride in the battle of Chancellorsville at Salem Church, stalling Sedgwick's advance. He had a small command and fought a gallant action. After Ewell's retirement, Early took a more active commanding role in the Army of Northern Virginia.

Later he was prominent in the Shenandoah campaigns, taking up where Jackson had left off. He even made it within miles of Washington, D.C. in 1864, after defeating Wallace at Monocacy; only the arrival of VI Corps chased him off. Custer destroyed the remnants of Early's unit in 1865 at the battle of Waynesboro. At the end of the war he fled to Mexico. Later he returned and became president of the Southern Historical Society. Early felt Longstreet was his enemy and never missed a chance to discredit him. Early was audacious and a tenacious fighter who was irascible and personally brave. Although not as perceptive as Lee or Jackson, and less effective in a solitary command role than as a subordinate, he was an effective officer. He died in 1894.

UNION COMMANDERS

Joseph Hooker

General Joseph (Fightin' Joe) Hooker is a figure of Shakespearean tragedy. With Lee's defeat within his grasp, he let it slip away because he lost faith in himself when Lee did not react predictably.

Hooker had risen through the efforts of his friends (including cabinet officer Salmon Chase) and through his own boastfulness. Often he resorted to self-aggrandizement or character assassination of his superiors in his quest for advancement, slandering them and anyone else he saw as a potential threat and gaining a deserved reputation as a malcontent. By boasting to Lincoln that he was superior to any Federal commanders at Bull Run in 1861, he acquired a command from Lincoln when General Scott refused to grant him one. Scott remembered Hooker's unprofessional conduct toward him from the Mexican-American War and still bore animosity toward Hooker.

Despite Lincoln's warnings that the Army of Northern Virginia was his target, Hooker felt that if he captured Richmond, the Southern capital, the Confederacy would sue for peace.

Hooker proved himself a brave and able commander in the following year, leading first a division and then I Corps. However, when Burnside undertook the assault across the Rappahannock on Fredericksburg, Hooker criticized him. Burnside was aware of Hooker's reputation as a malcontent and resolved to remove him from command when the opportunity presented itself. Hooker, however, fomented dissatisfaction among the corps' commanders, and two commanders went to Lincoln, complaining of Burnside's military ineptitude. Eventually Lincoln replaced Burnside with Hooker.

When he gave Hooker command of the Army of the Potomac, Lincoln warned him that his past behavior had made him no friends; in effect, he told Hooker that now he had no one but himself to blame if he did not succeed. Hooker boasted that he would take Richmond in 90 days.

Hooker is reputed to have been a hard drinker, almost a drunkard. Ironically, to some scholars, this bit of character assassination seems somewhat unfounded. Although Hooker did drink, some have speculated he was probably a man who could not hold his liquor well, and so appeared inebriated when he had had much less to drink than many others. Certainly he was no abstainer, but there is little other than hearsay to brand him as a drunkard. At Chancellorsville he was probably not drunk but shell-shocked; it is perhaps poetic justice that character assassination which helped him through the ranks also served to damn him in popular opinion.

Hooker reinvigorated the ailing Army of the Potomac, improving living conditions, building esprit de corps, and instituting the organizational structure it was to bear throughout the remainder of the war. He successfully placed his troops between Lee and both Washington and Baltimore, while holding Lee at bay, and gained the approbation of Congress for so doing.

As a commander, Hooker could formulate workable plans, but although he would set them in motion, he did not have the courage of his convictions to stick to a decided course of action. Unfortunately, Hooker was a general who had little real faith in his men or his plans, and like many other Union officers, he probably lionized Robert E. Lee; at Lee's faintest show of resistance, Hooker moved from an offensive to a defensive posture.

After Chancellorsville, Hooker was relieved. He was given command of XX Corps in the west and fought well in the Chattanooga campaign. He retired from active duty in 1868. Hooker was a man who aspired to greatness, and when given the chance, he was found wanting. He died in New York in 1879.

John Sedgwick

John Sedgwick graduated West Point in 1837 with classmates such as Bragg, Early, Hooker, and Pemberton. He served in the Seminole War, and served under Taylor in the Mexican-American War. In 1861 he was a major in the U.S. 1st Cavalry under the command of Lt.Col. Robert E. Lee. When Lee resigned to go with seceding Virginia, Sedgwick became the commander of the 1st Cavalry and was commissioned brigadier general of volunteers.

In the Peninsular War, he was wounded at Glendale. At Antietam he was noted for gallantry and was wounded three times, and carried unconscious from the field. His willingness to share the front line hardships with his men, his concern for their welfare, and his personal indifference to danger earned him the affectionate name of "Papa John" from his troops.

At Chancellorsville Sedgwick was given the thankless task of acting as a diversion for Hooker's main assault. He was promised reinforcements for his attack on the city, but they never materialized, so he cautiously advanced, fighting his way to Salem Church before wisely retiring to the river to cover the ford, thus preserving the Union left flank. Hooker tried to put blame for the failure on Sedgwick, but Washington realized that Sedgwick had done all that most commanders in the same situation could have done. Although VI Corps was held in reserve at Gettysburg and saw limited action, he commanded Union troops at Rappahannock and distinguished himself.

John Sedgwick, "Papa John" to his men, sat quiescent before Chancellorsville, only to break through and attempt to link up with Hooker, who abandoned him to his fate without a second thought.

In the Wilderness, his unit performed well, and at the battle of Spotsylvania, he was cut down by a Confederate sniper because he stood exposed, surveying the battle. Sedgwick was a thoroughly capable and professional soldier who earned the respect of his peers and those he commanded. His death diminished the Union pool of good officers, and had it occurred earlier, it may have hurt the Union cause.

O.O. Howard

Oliver Otis Howard was a deeply religious man who graduated from Bowdoin College in 1850 and West Point four years later. He taught at West Point as an assistant professor of mathematics. His career is an enigma, as he made many military blunders yet still advanced in rank.

Although his regiments at First Bull Run were driven from the field, he was promoted to brigadier-general. At Seven Pines during the Peninsular campaign, he lost his right arm while commanding a II Corps brigade. At Second Manassas he commanded the Federal rear guard; at Antietam he commanded 2nd Division, II Corps, after Sedgwick was wounded.

When Siegel asked to be removed from command of XI Corps, Howard was given that command, which was composed primarily of German troops. He failed to guard his flank (and the flank of the Army of the Potomac) at Chancellorsville, and was routed. At Gettysburg he was briefly in command of the field after Reynolds' death and before Hancock's arrival. His main contribution to the Union cause, however, was that he chose Cemetery Hill for the Union position.

Howard commanded XI and XII Corps under Hooker in the Chattanooga campaign and then commanded the IV Corps during the Atlanta campaign. Sherman appointed him commander of the Army of Tennessee in the Carolina campaign. At the end of the war he was appointed head of the Freedmen's Bureau by President Andrew Johnson. Although personally honest, Howard's bureau was rife with corruption, and he refused to see the faults and crimes of many of his subordinates.

Oliver Otis Howard lost his right arm and never allowed himself to be photographed as other than a bust shot. His negligence at Chancellorsville led to XI Corps' rout.

Meade was noted for his short temper. When Hooker stopped the army's advance and consolidated around Chancellorsville, Meade grumbled, "If he can't hold the top of the hill, how does he expect to hold the bottom of it?"

Exonerated in a court martial in 1874, he integrated a Congregational Church in Washington, D.C., founded Howard University in Washington, was active in the Indian Wars in the southwest, and was appointed superintendent of West Point. In 1893 he was awarded a Medal of Honor for his role at Seven Pines, and he died in 1909.

Howard was an honest man who overlooked flaws in others, and he did not appear to dabble in politics and petty jealousies. A mediocre commander, he appeared not to think deeply about situations, which led to his being surprised at Chancellorsville.

George Gordon Meade

Meade graduated from West Point in 1835 and served in Florida, but he resigned from service to become a civil engineer. In 1842 he petitioned the Army and was reinstated as a topographical engineer. Although he saw action in the Mexican-American War, Meade primarily served in the construction of lighthouses and coastal breakwaters thereafter.

When the Civil War began, Meade became commander of a Pennsylvania brigade and then helped to build the fortifications around Washington before he joined McClellan in the Peninsula. Tenacious, with a short fuse for officers who were incompetent, Meade proved himself to be an able leader who was admired by other officers for his accomplishments and professionalism. Wounded at Glendale, he recovered in time to lead his brigade at Second Manassas. At Antietam he commanded a I Corps division under Hooker. Under Franklin, he commanded 3rd division in I Corps where he was one of the few officers who captured and held a portion of the Confederate emplacements. He commanded V Corps at Chancellorsville, and had great success until Hooker ordered all commanders to stop their advance. Just prior to Gettysburg he was appointed to command the Army of the Potomac.

Although many felt Meade did not pursue Lee aggressively after Gettysburg, it is unlikely that the Army of the Potomac was really in any condition to do so. When newly appointed Lieutenant General Grant arrived in the east in 1864, he made his headquarters in the eastern theater with the Army of the Potomac. Meade retained immediate command of the Army of the Potomac throughout the remainder of the war, but he took his orders directly from Grant.

At the end of the war, Meade was promoted to major-general. He was given command of the Division of the Atlantic headquartered in Philadelphia. Meade was on active duty when he caught pneumonia and died in 1872.

John Reynolds

John F. Reynolds graduated from West Point in 1841. He served on the Texas frontier and in the Mexican-American War. In 1860 he was commandant of cadets at West Point. When war broke out, he was appointed lieutenant-colonel of the 14th United States Infantry.

In 1862 Reynolds was captured in the Peninsula, when McCall's division routed and his unit was overrun, but he was exchanged on 8 August 1862. At Second Manassas he commanded 3rd Division Pennsylvania Reserves. At Fredericksburg, he commanded I Corps in Frederick's Left Grand Division, and under his command, Meade accomplished one of the few bright spots of that day, when he gained and held a portion of the former Confederate line.

At Chancellorsville elements of Reynolds' command gained great headway, and they were stopped from pursuing Lee only by direct orders from Hooker. After Chancellorsville he was reportedly offered command of the Army of the Potomac, but he declined because he felt he would not be free to act as he thought best. When Meade was appointed commander of the Army of the Potomac, Reynolds followed his former subordinate's orders without complaint and led the advance elements of the army that occupied Gettysburg on 1 July 1863. Later that day he was killed while directing the efforts of the Iron Brigade against a Confederate onslaught.

Reynolds was a good soldier. At Chancellorsville he would lose patience when Hooker retreated without even closing to give Lee a real fight.

OPPOSING ARMIES

UNION TROOPS

The "90-Day War" was in its second year. The Union Army of the Potomac was on its fourth commander, Maj.Gen. Joseph Hooker. Although better equipped and superior in number to the Confederates, prior to Hooker's arrival the army suffered rock-bottom morale. Reporters and spies were telegraphing its every move both north and south of the Mason-Dixon line, it was in a cumbersome Grand Division structure, and the army had the feeling that even their victories were negated by the decisive actions of Stonewall Jackson and Robert E. Lee.

In their winter camps sanitation was poor; almost as many men were killed and sidelined by disease as by Confederate rifles. Men whose terms of enlistment were due to expire were reluctant to fight, the cavalry could not effectively meet Confederate cavalry, and although the area between the Rappahannock and the Potomac was nominally under Union control, Confederates could move readily through this area to strike at military targets. Vicksburg held out against the Union Army, and just months earlier, Southerners had thrust north to Antietam, where they were stopped by a fortuitous discovery of Lee's battle plans wrapped around three cigars. Even then the North could not savor a victory, for Hill's arrival had rescued Lee's army. The Army of Northern Virginia was a threat not only to Washington, but also to Pennsylvania.

Preliminary military fervor was ebbing, and although the Emancipation Proclamation had the effect of turning this war over states' rights from a war over a philosophical difference into a war with a real face – that of oppressed people held in bondage – many Northerners were opposed to the war and wanted to reach a negotiated settlement with the South. Such a settlement would mean a political, if not military, victory for the Confederacy. Lincoln's proclamation gave war-weary soldiers, who would just as soon have rid the United States of the Southern malcontents by letting them have a separate nation, a new reason to fight.

Congress enacted conscription laws to increase the Federal manpower pool. Soon draft riots would erupt in New York City and the "peace movement" would gain momentum as dead and wounded rolls in newspapers grew each week. Although they were not winning battles, the Union Army had changed since Bull Run, and they were now seasoned fighters, feeling that although they had "lost" at Antietam, they had done something grand in stopping Lee's unstoppable army and sending it tumbling back into Virginia.

The Union soldier was often a volunteer or a bounty-man who had been paid to take the service of another. Generally uniforms were prescribed by

These cavalrymen were the backbone of Stoneman's cavalry corps, yet their leader wasted them. However, fighting men like Lieutenant Colonel Duncan McVicar led them bravely against superior odds, showing Stuart that he was no longer the uncontested cavalry expert.

government regulations, but state units and local militia which had been "Federalized" kept unique accouterments. The Bucktails, for example, wore a buck's tail at the side of the kepi in the way many Confederate cavalrymen wore feathers. Although the Hardee hat, dark blue frock coat, and lighter blue trousers had been standard at the start of the war, by Chancellorsville the kepi was universally accepted and many units wore slouch hats whose wide brim protected the face and neck from snow, rain, and sun. Most infantrymen sported "sack" coats. These were more the length of today's suit coat, whereas the original issue frock coats were the length of 1860s mid-thigh length suit coats. Many infantry units were issued leggings (which were often discarded) in lieu of boots, and the most common footgear was the brogan – a heavy shoe. With these brogans troops wore thick, long, heavy socks which could be pulled up over the pant legs to mid-calf in winter or when moving through brush.

Cavalry usually wore kepis or slouch hats, and although a shell jacket was often worn, some units wore sack coats. Boots were universal. Artillerymen wore modified issue uniforms for either the cavalry (horse artillery) or infantry (foot artillery) uniforms. Generally speaking, the kepi was much more in evidence in the artillery than in either the infantry or the cavalry, despite regulations.

Hooker instituted a series of distinguishing unit insignia for corps within the Army of the Potomac. These were: circle, I Corps; clover, II Corps; diamond, III Corps; Maltese (Iron) Cross, V Corps; equilateral, straight-arm cross, VI Corps; crescent with opening to left, XI Corps; and five-pointed star with point up, XII Corps. Divisions within the corps were designated to use specific colors for the devices, with red for 1st Division, white for 2nd, and blue for 3rd. Facing colors were medium blue for infantry (as opposed to the almost black-navy blue), sunflower yellow for cavalry, grass green for medical, and bright fire-engine red for artillery. Trouser stripes, backing for officers' shoulder boards and epaulettes, enlisted men's stripes, and often guidons or colors bore these hues. (For additional details, refer to Osprey's American Civil War *Men At Arms* or *Warrior* series listed on the imprint page.)

Initially infantrymen were most often armed with an 1855 percussion rifled musket that shot a Minie ball and used the Maynard tape primer; however, the Maynard system proved ineffective, and as a result the weapons in use were refitted to accommodate individual cap primers. The 1855 Harper's Ferry smoothbore musket, which was similar, or the 1861 model Springfield, which used percussion primer caps, were adopted. Over 670,000 of the latter were used by Union forces. Weighing 8.88 lbs, measuring 55.75 inches, and using a .58 caliber ball, these rifles had an effective range of 500-600 yards. They were fitted with an 18 inch socket bayonet.

Some of the 1st New York artillery batteries were equipped with the 20 lb Parrott Rifle, a weapon which far surpassed many of the Confederates' older Napoleon guns.

This photograph of Capt. J.D. Smith shows the uniform of a Confederate artillery officer about mid-May 1863, with a nine-button shell jacket, knee boots, and kepi. Smith served in Jordan's battery under Alexander in Longstreet's corps.

Cavalrymen usually used a Colt .44 caliber six-shot percussion revolver or a six-shot .44 caliber Remington. The ball measured .46 for a .44 caliber pistol to insure tight seating on the powder load. They usually carried a single-shot Sharps 1859 .52 caliber breech-loading carbine, which weighed 7.9 lbs and was 39 inches long. In 1863 the Spencer repeating carbine was approved and introduced. It fired seven-shots, weighed 9.1 lbs. and measured 39 inches in length. The Spencer gave cavalry greater firepower, partly because of its multiple-round butt-loading magazine, but also because the metal cartridges held both primer and charge/bullet. Spencer rounds were just over an ounce, weighed 385 grains in .52 caliber, and used 48 grains of powder. The standard issue cavalry saber was either the older 'wrist-breaker' 1840 dragoon saber (straight-edge) or the 1860 light cavalry saber (curved edge), which measured 34 inches, had a finger guard and fitted in a heavy iron scabbard. Artillerymen used a short gladius-style sword (similar to that used by Napoleon's artillerymen), and were most often armed with standard Springfields, kept stacked away from the guns but within reach in case infantry or cavalry threatened to overrun the position. The 12 lb "Napoleon" smoothbore was the standard artillery piece, although batteries of 3 inch or 3.5 inch rifled guns were becoming more prevalent by the middle of the war.

Confederate troops

Confederate troops were underfed, armed with a motley mishmash of weapons and artillery, and poorly equipped, yet they had without question been the better fighting force since the war's inception.

Confederate supply and logistics were inferior to those of the Union, and uniform material was often in short supply. Soldiers were inspired with the belief that led by Bobby Lee, Stonewall Jackson, or Old Pete Longstreet, they could not lose. They accepted hunger, endured the cold and wet, and scrounged equipment from the dead or from that discarded on the battlefield by fleeing Union soldiers. Confederate soldiers in tattered butternut wore a motley array of Union shoes, trousers, overcoats, blankets, and web gear (and thus sometimes could be subject to friendly fire because other Confederate troops could not recognize them as fellow soldiers).

Confederate infantry wore gray, substituted by butternut when dye became in short supply as the war continued. They wore shorter sack coats, partly because this allowed better freedom of movement and partly because they conserved material by having shorter skirts. In the middle of the war many Southern supply depots began providing shell jackets with between seven and nine buttons. Although brogan shoes were supposed to be standard issue, in the summer many men went shoeless, since shoes were in short supply. Units' specifics varied according to state and whether they were regular Confederate troops as opposed to state troops or militia. In general, although kepis were worn, slouch hats were by far the most widely used headwear. This is because in the hot and rainy south, men learned the value of face and neck protection offered by the wide brims, and a wide brim provided shade for the eyes when aiming a rifle. Shades of gray varied, as did the trousers, which were sometimes gray, sometimes light blue, sometimes light gray, and often butternut or brown by late in the war. Although uniforms prescribed blue pants, as shortages increased, depots found it expedient to cut jackets and pants from the same material. Backing colors for collars, cuffs, and enlisted stripes were medium blue for infantry, red for artillery, loden gray-green for medical, mustard yellow for cavalry, and buff-medium khaki for staff officers.

The cavalry usually wore snappy shell jackets, boots, and reinforced trousers. Many cavalrymen and artillerymen wore similar shell jackets (with different facing colors) as the South often lacked the ability to mass-produce the variety of coats as the war wore on. As with the Union, brogan shoes with heavy socks often replaced boots. Leggings were rarely issued to Southern troops, and if a unit was fortunate enough to have them, they were rarely worn after First Manassas, when the regular soldier learned to differentiate which equipment was essential and which was merely heavy. Southerners favored blanket rolls and haversacks with canteens instead of backpacks, although some units who had backpacks retained them.

The favorite sidearms were Federal issue. The infantry standard rifle was the 1855 Harper's Ferry model .58 caliber musket or the re-rifled 1840 Mississippi .54 caliber rifles which became .58 caliber pieces. Also common were the 1842 Palmetto South Carolina .69 caliber smoothbore percussion musket (copy of U.S. Model 1842 musket), the .58 calibre Eli Whitney Enfield musket (all purchased before the 1861 arms embargo), and the 1853 .577 Enfield rifled musket (standard British issue) imported from England. Most used an 18 inch socket bayonet. The cavalry used sabers (generally dragoon straight or light cavalry curved copies), and some carried massive Bowie-knives, which were almost as big as boarding cutlasses. As the cavalry tradition of saber-charges was rapidly waning, the South seemed to discard the saber as a standard weapon in favour of rifles, carbines, pistols and sawed-off shotguns early in the war, whereas the Union retained the saber as standard issue.

Many Southern cavalry carried one or more pistols, often Colt .44 caliber six-shot revolvers or Spiller & Burr copies of the Federal Whitney .36 caliber six-shot revolver. Carbines used included the Richmond Sharps .52 caliber breechloader, the early model Maynard break-breech carbine (in both .35 and .50 calibers which used rounds with ball, charge, and primer in a metal casing), the Colt six-shot repeating percussion carbine (in .36, .44, and .56 calibres), and the 39 inch long .58 caliber Richmond Carbine, which copied the Harper's Ferry U.S. carbine from early in the war.

Cavalry shotguns were generally double-barreled 12-gauge percussion shotguns with the barrels sawed off to make the gun around 30 inches long. With these, one Confederate regiment is reported to have scattered 400 Yankee troopers which three previous charges by regiments had failed to break. Often Confederates armed themselves with foraged Union weapons, but with some, such as the Sharps, scarce ammunition proved to be a headache for the common soldier.

Confederate artillery was a mixed bag, and whereas many Union units had guns all of the same make and caliber, Southern units were often equipped with mixed guns, both rifled and smoothbores of widely varied calibers. Still most common were the 12 lb smoothbore Napoleons, although 6 lb brass smoothbores were frequently used in the South. Other common guns were the 10 lb field rifle, the 12 lb howitzer, and the highly prized 12 lb Whitworth breechloading rifle (made in England).

Supplies were low. Southern cities felt supply shortages, and some 12-month men, who had signed up after First Manassas, had gone home. However, the nucleus of the army, the hard fighting men, were still an impenetrable line south and west of the Rappahannock. They wore ragged blankets if they had no overcoats, they drank chicory mixed with coffee and fried crackers in bacon grease, and they often lived off greens and food foraged or hunted because government issue was slow and irregular. (For more details, see Osprey's Warrior 6: *Confederate Infantryman 1861-1865*, or the Men-at-Arms series of American Civil War books.)

Southern soldiers' faces were gaunt, but their lips were set in a tight line beneath eyes as bright as their carefully cleaned and oiled rifles. These men appreciated the battle-fever they saw in Thomas J. Jackson's eyes when they nicknamed him "Ole Blue Light" or spoke with admiration of his tenacity and derring-do when they called him "That Crazy Old Presbyterian Fool." If he was a crazy fool, he was a victorious crazy fool, and most importantly, he was the crazy fool who made them a fearsome fighting machine.

Taken in mid-April 1863, this shows Stonewall Jackson as thinner and more tired than a year earlier. Two weeks later this "crazy Presbyterian fool" would march circles around Hooker to rout XI Corps.

Units present are followed by their commander's rank and name, and their estimated effective strength at the start of the first day of battle (or actual available for duty strength if available and documented by the National Archives' day reports); in the case of artillery, the number of troops is followed by the number and kind of guns. Numbers of troops shown in parentheses () are taken from national archives or other state sources: bracketed numbers {} are taken from related sources such as quarter master records and are extrapolated to determine how many men were probably available on active duty.

ABBREVIATIONS

Abbreviations of rank: **Maj.Gen.**=Major General, **Lt.Gen.**=Lieutenant General, **Brig.Gen.**=Brigadier General, **Col.**=Colonel, **Lt.Col.**=Lieutenant Colonel, **Maj.**=Major, **Capt.**=Captain, **1stLt.**=1st Lieutenant, and **2nd Lt**=2nd Lieutenant.

Abbreviations for types of artillery pieces are: **N**=Napoleon gun, **6G**=6lb. field gun, **10H**=10lb. howitzer, **12H**=12lb. howitzer, **20H**=20lb. howitzer, **24H**=24lb. howitzer, **3R**=3-inch rifle, **4.5R**=4.5-inch rifle, **10P**=10lb. Parrott rifle, **20P**=20lb. Parrott rifle, **JR**=James Rifle, **W**=Whitworth gun, **BR**=Blakely Rifle, **3NR**=3-inch Navy Rifle

---

28 APRIL – 6 MAY, 1863

ARMY OF THE POTOMAC

Maj.Gen. Joseph (Fightin' Joe) Hooker (130,576)

General HQ (1,971)
Staff: 67

Provost Marshal General – Brig.Gen. Marsena R. Patrick (952)
93rd New York – Col. John S. Crocker (309)
E&I 6th Pennsylvania Cavalry – Capt. James Starr (137)
A,B,C,D,F,G 8th US Infantry – Capt. Edwin H. Reed (464)
US Cavalry Detachment – 1st Lt. Tatnall Paulding {42}

PATRICK'S BRIGADE
Col. Wm. F. Rogers (2,097)
B/Maryland Light Artillery – Capt. Alonzo Snow {102} (4/12N)
12th Btty/Ohio Light Artillery – Capt. Aaron C. Johnson (121) (6/12N)
21st New York – Lt.Col. Chester W. Sternberg (362)
23rd New York – Col. Henry C. Hoffman (521)
35th New York – Col. John G. Todd (622)
80th New York (20th Militia) – Col. Theodore B. Gates (369)

ENGINEER BRIGADE
Brig.Gen. Henry W. Benham (1,277)
Staff: 4
15th New York – Col. Clinton G. Colgate (126)
50th New York – Col. Charles B. Stuart (479)
US Battalion – Capt. Chauncey B. Reese (419)

Signal Corps – Capt. Samuel T. Cushing (202)
Balloon Corps – Professor Thaddeus S.C. Lowe (2)
Ordnance Detachment – 1st Lt. John R. Edie (45)

ARTILLERY

Brig.Gen. Henry J. Hunt (Hooker placed him in nominal command, but did not allow him to coordinate artillery fire during main battle.)

ARTILLERY RESERVE

Brig.Gen. Robert O. Tyler (1,347)
Escort – Ist Co./1st Maine Cavalry – Capt. Constantine Taylor (32)
Staff: 4

B/1st Connecticut Heavy Arty – 1st Lt. Albert F. Brooker (110) (4/4.5)
M/1st Connecticut Heavy Arty – Capt. Franklin A. Pratt (110) (4/4.5)
5th Btty New York Light Arty – Capt. Elijah D. Taft (146) (6/20P)
15th Btty New York Light Arty – Capt. Patrick Hart (70) (4/12N)
29th Btty New York Light Arty – 1st Lt. Gustav von Blucher (90) (4/20P)
30th Btty New York Light Arty – Capt. Adolph Voegelee (124) (6/20P)
32nd Btty New York Light Arty – 1st Lt. George Gaston (122) (6/3R)
K/1st US Arty – 1st Lt. Lorenzo Thomas Jr. (114) (6/3R)
C/3rd US Arty – 1st Lt. Henry Meinell (142) (6/3R)
G/4th US Arty – 1st Lt. Marcus P. Miller (122) (6/12N)
K/5th US Arty – 1st Lt. David H. Kinzie (113) (4/12N)
C/32nd Massachusetts Inf. – Capt. Josiah C. Fuller (48)

I CORPS

Maj.Gen. John F. Reynolds (17,070)
Staff: 14

1ST DIVISION

Brig.Gen. James S. Wadsworth (9,100)
Staff: 11

1ST BRIGADE
Col. Walter J. Phelps Jr. (1,725)
Staff: 15
22nd New York – Maj. Thomas J. Strong (576)
24th New York – Col. Samuel R. Beardsley (300)
30th New York – Col. William M. Searing {493}
84th New York – Col. Edw. B. Fowler (341)

2ND BRIGADE
Brig.Gen. Lysander Cutler (1,773)
Staff: 8
7th Indiana – Col. Ira G. Grover (437)
76th New York – Col. William P. Wainwright (375)
95th New York – Col. Geo. H. Biddle (261)
147th New York – Col. John G. Butler (430)
56th Pennsylvania – Col. J. Wm. Hoffman (262)

3RD BRIGADE
Brig.Gen. Gabriel R. Paul (3,385)
Staff: 4
22nd New Jersey – Col. Abraham G. Demarest (704)
29th New Jersey – Col. Wm. R. Taylor (633)
30th New Jersey – Col. John I. Cladek (703)
31st New Jersey – Lt.Col. Robert R. Honeyman (698)
137th Pennsylvania – Col. Joseph B. Kiddoo (643)

4TH BRIGADE
Brig.Gen. Solomon Meredith (1,873)
Staff: 2

19th Indiana – Col. Samuel J. Williams (339)
24th Michigan – Col. Henry A. Morrow (496)
2nd Wisconsin – Col. Lucius Fairchild (321)
6th Wisconsin – Col. Edward S. Bragg (342)
7th Wisconsin – Col. Wm. W. Robinson (373)

1ST DIVISION ARTILLERY

Capt. John A. Reynolds (333)
Staff: 2
A/1st Btty/New Hampshire Light Arty – Capt. Frederick M. Edgell (80) (6/3R)
L/1st New York Light Arty – Capt. John A. Reynolds (125) (6/3R)
B/4th US Arty – 1st Lt. James Stewart (126) (6/12N)

2ND DIVISION

Brig.Gen. John C. Robinson (4,820)
Staff: 13

1ST BRIGADE

Col. Adrian R. Root (1,170)
Staff: 4
16th Maine – Col. Charles W. Tilden (311)
94th New York – Capt. Samuel A. Moffett (262)
104th New York – Col. Gilbert G. Prey (312)
107th Pennsylvania – Col. Thomas F. McCoy (281)

2ND BRIGADE

Brig.Gen. Henry Baxter (1,786)
Staff: 4
12th Massachusetts – Col. James L. Bates (269)
26th New York – Lt.Col. Gilbert S. Jennings (784)
90th Pennsylvania – Col. Peter Lyle (216)
136th Pennsylvania – Col. Thomas M. Bayne (513)

3RD BRIGADE

Col. Samuel H. Leonard (1,320)
Staff: 11
13th Massachusetts – Lt.Col. Walter N. Batchelder (302)
83rd New York (9th Militia) – Lt.Col. Joseph Anton Moesch (206)
97th New York – Col. Charles Wheelock (255)
11th Pennsylvania – Col. Richard Coulter (270)
88th Pennsylvania – Lt.Col. Louis Wagner (276)

ARTILLERY

Capt. Dunbar R. Ransom (531)
Staff: 2
B/2nd Btty/Maine Light Arty – Capt. James A. Hall (127) (6/3R)
E/5th Btty/Maine Light Arty – Capt. George F. Lieppen (164) (5/12N)
C/Pennsylvania Light Arty – Capt. James Thompson (109) (4/10lb)
C/5th US Arty – Capt. Dunbar R. Ransom (129) (6/12N)

3RD DIVISION

Maj.Gen. Abner Doubleday (3,136)
Staff: 13

1ST BRIGADE

Brig.Gen. Thomas A. Rowley (1,435)
Staff: 2
121st Pennsylvania – Col. Chapman Biddle (266)

135th Pennsylvania – Col. James R. Porter (684)
151st Pennsylvania – Col. Harrison Allen (483)

2ND BRIGADE

Col. Roy Stone (1,320)
Staff: 2
143rd Pennsylvania – Col. Edmund L. Dana (466)
149th Pennsylvania – Lt.Col. Dalton Wight (451)
150th Pennsylvania – Col. Langhorne Wister (401)

ARTILLERY

Maj. Ezra W. Matthews (368)
Staff: 2
B/1st Pennsylvania Light Arty – Capt. James H. Cooper (106) (4/3R)
F/1st Pennsylvania Light Arty – 1st Lt. R. Bruce Ricketts (105) (4/3R)
G/1st Pennsylvania Light Arty (Combined) – Capt. Frank P. Amsden (155) (8/3R)

II CORPS

Maj.Gen. Darius N. Couch (14,638)
Staff: 6

Escort: D&F/6th New York Cavalry – Capt. Riley Johnson (67)
Chief of Artillery – Lt.Col. Charles H. Morgan

1ST DIVISION

MG Winfield S. Hancock (4,732)
Staff: 4

1ST BRIGADE

Brig.Gen. John C. Caldwell (980)
Staff. 7
61st New York – Col. Nelson A. Miles (202)
66th New York – Col. Orlando H. Morris (217)
148th Pennsylvania – Col. James A. Beaver (556)

2ND BRIGADE

Brig.Gen. Thomas F. Meagher (562)
Staff: 5
28th Massachusetts – Col. Richard Byrnes (240)
63rd New York – Lt.Col. Richard C. Bentley (118)
69th New York – Capt. James E. McGee (85)
116th Pennsylvania Battalion – Maj. St. Clair Augustin Mulholland (114)

3RD BRIGADE

Brig.Gen. Samuel K. Zook (950)
Staff: 4
52nd New York – Col. Paul Frank (177)
57th New York – Lt.Col. Alford B. Chapman (210)
140th Pennsylvania – Col. Richard P. Roberts (559)

4TH BRIGADE

Col. John R. Brooke (1,402)
Staff: 6
27th Connecticut – Col. Richard S. Bostwick (291)

2nd Delaware – Lt.Col. David L. Sticker (341)
64th New York – Col. Daniel G. Bingham (265)
53rd Pennsylvania – Lt.Col. Richards McMichael (175)
145th Pennsylvania – Col. Hiram L. Brown (324)

5TH BRIGADE (ATTACHED)

Col. Edward E. Cross (580)
Staff: 4
5th NH – Lt.Col. Charles E. Hapgood (204)
81st PA – Col. H. Boyd McKeen (236)
88th New York – Col. Patrick Kelly (136)

ARTILLERY

Capt. Rufus D. Pettit (254)
Staff: 2
B/New York Light Arty – Capt. Rufus D. Pettit (126) (6/3R)
C/4th US Arty – 1st Lt. Evan Thomas (126) (6/12N)

2ND DIVISION

Brig.Gen. John Gibbon (4,800)
Staff: 6

1ST BRIGADE

Brig.Gen. Alfred Sully (1,762)
Staff: 8
19th Maine – Col. Francis E. Heath (439)
15th Massachusetts – Maj. George C. Joslin (245)
1st Minnesota – Lt.Col. William Colvill Jr. (339)
34th New York – Col. Byron Laflin (390)
82nd New York (2nd Militia) – Col. Henry W. Hudson/Lt.Col. James Houston (341)

2ND BRIGADE

Brig.Gen. Joshua T. Owen (1,208)
Staff: 3
69th Pennsylvania – Col. Dennis O'Kane (284)
71st Pennsylvania – Col. Richard P. Smith (261)
72nd Pennsylvania – Col. Dewitt C. Baxter (380)
106th Pennsylvania – Col. Turner G. Morehead (280)

3RD BRIGADE

Col. Norman J. Hall (1,528)
Staff: 3
19th Massachusetts – Col. Arthur Devereaux (172)
20th Massachusetts – Lt.Col. George N. Macy (260)
7th Michigan – Lt.Col. Amos Steele (172)
42nd New York – Col. James E. Mallon (206)
59th New York – Lt.Col. Max A. Thomond (187)
127th Pennsylvania – Col. Wm. W. Jennings (528)

ARTILLERY (246)

A/1st Rhode Island Light Arty – Capt. Wm. A. Arnold (117) (6/3R)
B/1st Rhode Island Light Arty – 1st Lt. T. Frederick Brown (129) (6/12N)

Attached: **1st Co. Massachusetts Sharpshooters** – Capt. William Plumer (50)

3RD DIVISION

Maj.Gen. William H. French (5,033)
Staff: 8

Provost Guard – **10th New York/4 Co.** – Maj. G.F. Hopper {82}

1ST BRIGADE
Col. Samuel S. Carroll (2,009)
Staff: 7
14th Indiana – Col. John Coons (255)
24th New Jersey – Col. Wm. B. Robertson (460)
28th New Jersey – Lt.Col. John A. Wildrick (435)
4th Ohio – Lt.Col. Leonard W. Carpenter (372)
8th Ohio – Lt.Col. Franklin Sawyer (221)
7th West Virginia – Lt.Col. Joseph Snider (259)

2ND BRIGADE
Brig.Gen. William Hays (1,508)
Staff: 2
14th Connecticut – Maj. Theodore G. Ellis (228)
12th New Jersey – Col. J. Howard Willets (622)
108th New York – Col. Charles J. Powers (252)
130th Pennsylvania – Col. Levi Maish (404)

3RD BRIGADE
Col. John D. MacGregor (951)
Staff: 2
1st Delaware – Col. Thomas A. Smith (306)
4th New York – Lt.Col. Wm. Jameson (418)
132nd Pennsylvania – Col. Charles Albright (225)

ARTILLERY (237)
C/1st New York Light – 1st Lt. Nelson Ames (88) (6/3R)
G/1st Rhode Island Light – Capt. George W. Adams (149) (6/10P)

II CORPS ARTILLERY RESERVE (238)
I/1st US – 1st Lt. Kirby (112) (6/N)
A/4th US – 1st Lt. Cushing (126) (6/3R)

III CORPS

Maj.Gen. Daniel E. Sickles (17,607)
Chief of Artillery – Capt. George E. Randolph
Staff: 9

1ST DIVISION

Brig.Gen. David B. Birney (7,293)
Staff: 4

1ST BRIGADE
Brig.Gen. Charles K. Graham (2,275)
Staff: 4
57th Pennsylvania – Col. Peter Sides (278)
63rd Pennsylvania – Lt.Col. Wm. S. Kirkwood (364)
68th Pennsylvania – Col. Andrew H. Tippin (395)
105th Pennsylvania – Col. Amor A. McKnight (350)
114th Pennsylvania – Col. Charles Collis (440)
141st Pennsylvania – Col. Henry J. Madill (444)

2ND BRIGADE
Brig.Gen. J.H. Hobart Ward (2,156)
Staff: 6

20th Indiana – Col. John Wheeler (425)
3rd Maine – Col. Moses B. Lakeman (273)
4th Maine – Col. Elijah Walker (315)
38th New York – Col. Regis de Trobriand (333)
40th New York (Mozart Regt.) – Col. Thomas W. Egan (501)
99th Pennsylvania – Col. Asher S. Leidy (303)

3RD BRIGADE
Col. Samuel B. Hayman (2,482)
Staff: 1
17th Maine – Lt.Col. Charles Merrill (463)
3rd Michigan – Col. Byron R. Pierce (310)
5th Michigan – Maj. John Pulford (294)
1st New York – Lt.Col. Francis L. Leland (680)
37th New York – Lt.Col. Gilbert Riorden (734)

ARTILLERY
Capt. Judson A. Clark (376)
B/New Jersey Light Arty – 1st Lt. Rob't Sims/Capt. Adoniram B. Clark (153) (6/10P)
E/1st Rhode Island Light Arty – 1st Lt. Pardon S. Jastrom (108) (6/12N)
F&K/3rd US Arty – 1st Lt. John G. Turnbull (115) (6/12N)

2ND DIVISION

Maj.Gen. Hiram G. Berry (Brig.Gen. Joseph B. Carr) (6,699)
Staff: 4

1ST BRIGADE
Brig.Gen. Joseph B. Carr / Col. William Blaisdale (1,998)
Staff: 2
1st Massachusetts – Col. Napoleon B. McLaughlen (416)
11th Massachusetts – Col. Wm. Blaisdell (362)
16th Massachusetts – Lt.Col. Waldo Merriam (318)
11th New Jersey – Col. Robert McAllister (444)
26th Pennsylvania – Col. Benjamin C. Tilghman (456)

2ND BRIGADE
Brig.Gen. Joseph W. Revere (2,153)
Staff: 3
70th New York – Col. J. E. Farnum (320)
71st New York – Col. Henry L. Potter (282)
72nd New York – Col. Wm. O. Stevens (406)
73rd New York – Maj. Michael Wm. Burns (387)
74th New York – Lt.Col. Wm. H. Lounsbury (306)
120th New York – Lt.Col. Cornelius D. Westbrook (449)

3RD BRIGADE
Brig.Gen. Gershom Mott (2,123)
Staff: 2
5th New Jersey – Col. Wm. J. Sewell (327)
6th New Jersey – Col. George C. Burling (274)
7th New Jersey – Col. Louis R. Francine (322)
8th New Jersey – Col. John Ramsey (295)
2nd New York – Col. Sidney W. Park (641)
115th Pennsylvania – Col. Francis A. Lancaster (262)

ARTILLERY
Capt. Thomas W. Osborn (421)
Staff: 4
D/1st New York Light Arty – 1st Lt. George B. Winslow (116) (6/12N)
H/1st US Arty – 1st Lt. Justin F. Dimick (122) (6/12N)

K/4th US Arty – 1st Lt. Francis Seeley (179) (6/12N)

3RD DIVISION

Maj.Gen. Amiel W. Whipple (3,606)
Staff: 3

1ST BRIGADE
Col. Emlen Franklin (1,446)
Staff: 4
86th New York – Lt.Col. B. J. Chapin (364)
124th New York – Col. Augustus Van Horn Ellis (442)
122nd Pennsylvania – Lt.Col. Edward McGovern (636)

2ND BRIGADE
Col. Samuel M. Bowman (1,197)
Staff: 4
12th New Hampshire – Col. Joseph H. Potter (541)
84th Pennsylvania – Lt.Col. Milton Opp (455)
110th Pennsylvania – Col. James Crowther (197)

3RD BRIGADE
Col. Hiram Berdan (568)
Staff: 2
1st US Sharpshooters – Lt.Col. Casper Trepp (381)
2nd US Sharpshooters – Maj. Homer R. Stoughton (185)

ARTILLERY
Capt. Albert A. Von Puttkammer/Capt. James F. Huntington (392)
Staff: 2
10th Btty/New York Light Arty – 1st Lt. Samuel Lewis (116) (6/12N)
11th Btty/New York Light Arty – 1st Lt. J.E. Burton (149) (6/3R)
H/1st Ohio Light Arty – Capt. James F. Huntington (125) (6/3R)

V CORPS

Maj.Gen. George G. Meade (16,255)
Chief of Artillery – Capt. Stephen H. Weed
Staff: 7

Escort – **2 /17th PA Cavalry** – Capt. Wm. Thompson (448)

1ST DIVISION

Brig.Gen. Charles Griffin (6,690)
Staff: 4

1ST BRIGADE
Brig.Gen. James Barnes (2,180)
Staff: 1
2nd Maine – Col. George Varney (522)
18th Massachusetts – Col. Joseph Hayes (294)
22nd Massachusetts – Col. William S. Tilton (138)
1st Michigan – Col. Ira C. Abbott (160)
13th New York Battalion – Capt. Wm. Downey (544)
25th New York – Col. Charles H. Johnson (280)
118th Pennsylvania – Col. Charles P. Prevost (241)

2ND BRIGADE
Col. James McQuade (2,088)
Staff: 1
9th Massachusetts – Col. Patrick R. Guiney (425)
32nd Massachusetts – Lt.Col. Luther Stevenson (253)
4th Michigan – Col. Harrison H. Jeffords (362)
14th New York – Lt.Col. Thomas M Davies (606)
62nd Pennsylvania – Col. Jacob B. Sweitzer (441)

3RD BRIGADE
Col. Thomas W. Stockton (1,863)
Staff: 1
20th Maine – Lt.Col. Joshua Chamberlain (386)
16th Michigan – Lt.Col. Norval E. Welch (270)
Michigan Sharpshooters (attached to 16th Michigan) – Capt. Brady {53}
12th New York – Capt. William Huson (117)
17th New York – Lt.Col. Nelson B. Bartram (342)
44th New York – Col. James C. Rice (395)
83rd Pennsylvania – Col. Strong Vincent (299)

ARTILLERY
Capt. Augustus P. Martin (555)
Staff: 2
C (3rd Btty)/Massachusetts Light Arty – 1st Lt. Aaron F. Walcott (124) (6/12N)
E (5th Btty)/Massachusetts Light – Capt. Charles A. Phillips (104) (6/3R)
C/1st Rhode Island Light Arty – Capt. Richard Waterman (133) (6/3R)
D/5th US Arty – 1st Lt. Charles E. Hazlett (192) (6/12N)

2ND DIVISION

Maj.Gen. George Sykes (4,781)
Staff: 4

1ST BRIGADE
Brig.Gen. Romeyn B. Ayres (1,454)
Staff: 2
B,C,F,G,I,K/3rd US Inf. – Capt. John D. Wilkins (309)
C,F,H,K/4th US Inf. – Capt. Hiram Dryer (177)
A,B,C,D,G/1st Battalion/12th US Inf. – Maj. Richard S. Smith – (438)
A,B,C/2nd Battalion/12th US Inf. – (incl. above)
A,B,D,E,F,G/1st Battalion/14th US Inf. – Capt. Jonathan B. Hager (528)
F&G/2nd Battalion/14th US Inf. – Maj. Grotius R. Giddings (incl. above)

2ND BRIGADE
Col. Sidney Burbank (1,251)
Staff: 2
B,C,F,I,K/2nd US Inf. – Capt. Salem S. Marsh (225)
D,F,G,H,I/6th US Inf. – Capt. Levi C. Bootes (178)
A,B,E,I/7th US Inf. – Capt. David P. Hancock (132)
D,G & H/10th US Inf. – 1st Lt. Edward G. Bush (105)
B,C,D,E,F,G/1st Battalion/11th US Inf. – Maj. Delancey Floyd-Jones (314)
C&D/2nd Battalion/11th US Inf. – (incl. above)
A,C,D,G,H/1st Battalion/17th US Inf. – Maj. George L. Andrews (295)
A&B/2nd Battalion/17th US Inf. – (incl. above)

3RD BRIGADE
Col. Patrick H. O'Rorke (1,870)
Staff: 4
5th New York (Duryea's Zouaves) – Col. Cleveland Winslow (735)

140th New York – Lt.Col. Lewis Ernst (547)
146th New York – Col. Kenner Gerrard (584)

ARTILLERY
Capt. Steven H. Weed (202)
Staff: 2
L/1st Ohio Light Arty – Capt. Frank C. Gibbs (124) (6/12N)
I/5th US Arty – 1st Lt. Malbone F. Watson (76) (4/3R)

3RD DIVISION

Brig.Gen. Andrew H. Humphrey (4,329)
Staff: 5

1ST BRIGADE
Brig.Gen. Erastus B. Tyler (2,011)
Staff: 1
91st Pennsylvania – Col. Edward M. Gregory (296)
126th Pennsylvania – Lt.Col. David W. Rowe (581)
129th Pennsylvania – Col. Jacob G. Frick (592)
134th Pennsylvania – Col. Edward O'Brien (541)

2ND BRIGADE
Col. Peter H. Allabach (2,139)
Staff: 2
123rd Pennsylvania – Col. John B. Clark (675)
131st Pennsylvania – Maj. Robert W. Patton (510)
133rd Pennsylvania – Col. Franklin B. Speakman (576)
155th Pennsylvania – Lt.Col. John H. Cain (376)

ARTILLERY
Capt. Alanson M. Randol (174)
Staff: 2
C/1st New York Light Arty – Capt. Almont Barnes (88) (4/3R)
E&G/1st US Arty – Capt. Alanson M. Randol (84) (4/12N)

VI CORPS

Maj.Gen. John Sedgwick (22,968)
Staff: 13
Escort – Maj. Hugh H. Janeway
1 Co/1st NJ Cav – 1st Lt. Voorhees Dye (32)
1 Co/1st PA Cav – Capt. Wm. S. Craft (54)

1ST DIVISION

Brig.Gen. Wm. T.H. Brooks (8,068)
Staff: 6
Provost Guard – **3 cos./4th New Jersey** – Capt. Charles Ewing {86}

1ST BRIGADE
Col. Henry W. Brown (2,260)
Staff: 6
1st New Jersey – Col. Mark Collet (358)
2nd New Jersey – Col. Samuel L. Buck (406)
3rd New Jersey – Maj. J.W.H. Stickney (377)
15th New Jersey – Col. Wm. H. Penrose (564)
23rd New Jersey – Col. E. Burd Grubb (549)

2ND BRIGADE
Brig.Gen. Joseph J. Bartlett (2,879)
Staff: 4
5th Maine – Col. Clark S. Edwards (389)
16th New York – Col. Joel J. Seaver (745)
27th New York – Col. Alexander D. Adams (667)
121st New York – Col. Emory Upton (686)
96th Pennsylvania – Col. Wm. Lessig (388)

3RD BRIGADE
Brig.Gen. David A. Russell (2,363)
Staff: 6
18th New York – Col. George R. Myers (486)
32nd New York – Col. Francis E. Pinto (591)
49th Pennsylvania – Lt.Col. Thomas H. Hulings (285)
95th Pennsylvania – Col. Gustavus W. Town (465)
119th Pennsylvania – Col. Peter C. Ellmaker (530)

ARTILLERY
Maj. John A. Thompkins (474)
Staff: 2
A/1st Massachusetts Light Arty – Capt. William H. McCartney (137) (6/12N)
A/New Jersey Light Arty – 1st Lt. Augustin N. Parsons (99) (6/10P)
A/1st Maryland Light Arty – Capt. James H. Rigby (109) (6/3R)
D/2nd US Arty – 1st Lt. Edward B. Williston (127) (6/12N)

2ND DIVISION

Brig.Gen. Albion P. Howe (5,602)
Staff: 3

1ST BRIGADE
None present

2ND BRIGADE
Col. Lewis A. Grant (2,610)
Staff: 6
26th New Jersey – Col. Andrew J. Morrison (481)
2nd Vermont – Col. James H. Walbridge (576)
3rd Vermont – Col. Thomas O. Seaver (390)
4th Vermont – Col. Charles B. Stoughton (434)
5th Vermont – Lt.Col. John R. Lewis (318)
6th Vermont – Col. Elisha L. Barney (405)

3RD BRIGADE
Brig.Gen. Thomas H. Neill (2,759)
Staff: 16
7th Maine – Lt.Col. Seldon Connor (308)
21st New Jersey – Col. Gilliam Van Houten (739)
20th New York – Col. Ernst von Vegesack (570)
33rd New York – Col. Robert F. Taylor (281)
49th New York – Capt. Daniel D. Bidwell (394)
77th New York – Lt.Col. Windsor B. French (451)

ARTILLERY
Maj. J. Watts de Peyster (230)
Staff: 2
1st Btty/New York Light Arty – Capt. Andrew Cowan (103) (6/3R)
F/5th US Arty – 1st Lt. Leonard Martin (125) (6/10P)

3RD DIVISION

MG John Newton (6,172)
Staff: 3

1ST BRIGADE

Col. Alexander Shaler (1,930)
Staff: 3
65th New York – Lt.Col. Joseph E. Hamblin (294)
67th New York – Col. Nelson Cross (378)
122nd New York – Col. Silas Titus (403)
23rd Pennsylvania – Col. John Ely (528)
82nd Pennsylvania – Maj. Isaac G. Bassett (324)

2ND BRIGADE

Col. William H. Browne (2,154)
Staff: 1
7th Massachusetts – Lt.Col. Franklin P. Harlow (470)
10th Massachusetts – Lt.Col. Joseph B. Parsons (430)
37th Massachusetts – Col. Oliver Edwards (581)
36th New York – Lt.Col. James J. Walsh (243)
2nd Rhode Island – Col. Horatio Rogers Jr. (429)

3RD BRIGADE

Brig.Gen. Frank Wheaton (1,854)
Staff: 1
62nd New York – Col. David J. Nevin (357)
93rd Pennsylvania – Capt. John S. Long (313)
98th Pennsylvania – Capt. John F. Ballier (392)
102nd Pennsylvania – Col. Joseph M. Kinkead (272)
139th Pennsylvania – Col. Frederick H. Collier (519)

ARTILLERY

Capt. Jeremiah McCarthy (231)
Staff: 2
C&D/1st Pennsylvania Light Arty – Capt. Jeremiah M. McCarthy (114) (6/10P)
G/2nd US Arty – 1st Lt. John H. Butler (115) (6/12N)

LIGHT DIVISION

Brig.Gen. Calvin E. Pratt/Col. Hiram Burnham (3,027)
Staff: 2
6th Maine – Lt.Col. Benjamin F. Harris (547)
31st New York – Col. Frank Jones (705)
43rd New York – Col. Benjamin F. Baker (574)
61st Pennsylvania – Col. George C. Spear (474)
5th Wisconsin – Col. Thomas Allen (613)
3rd/New York Light Arty – 1st Lt. William A. Harn (112) (6/10P)

XI CORPS

Maj.Gen. Oliver O. Howard (11,924)
Staff: 11
Escort –**1st Indiana Cavalry, 2 Cos.** – Capt. Abram Sharra (120)

1ST DIVISION

Brig.Gen. Charles Devens Jr./ Brig.Gen. Daniel C. McLean (4,048)
Staff: 4

1ST BRIGADE

Col. Leopold von Gilsa (1,528)
Staff: 2
41st New York – Lt.Col. Heinrich D. Von Einsiede (279)
45th New York – Col. Geo. Von Amsburg (451)
54th New York – Maj.Steven Kovacs (232)
153rd Pennsylvania – Maj.Owen Rice (564)

2ND BRIGADE

Brig.Gen. Nathaniel C. McLean (2,353)
Staff: 4
17th Connecticut – Lt.Col. Douglas Fowler (497)
25th Ohio – Lt.Col. Jeremiah Williams (372)
55th Ohio – Col. Charles B. Gambee (480)
75th Ohio – Col. Andrew L. Harris (409)
107th Ohio – Capt. John M. Lutz (591)

UNATTACHED

Co./8th New York – 1st Lt. Hermann Rosenkranz {40}

ARTILLERY

Capt. Julius Dieckmann
13th Btty New York Light Arty – Capt. Julius Dieckmann (123) (6/3R)

2ND DIVISION

Brig.Gen. Adolph von Steinwehr (3,314)
Staff: 5

1ST BRIGADE

Col. Adolphus Buschbeck (1,420)
Staff: 5
29th New York – 1st Lt. Hans Von Brandis (132)
154th New York – Lt.Col. Daniel B. Allen (440)
27th Pennsylvania – Lt.Col. Lorenz Cantador (450)
73rd Pennsylvania – Lt.Col. Wiliam Moore (393)

2ND BRIGADE

Brig.Gen. Francis C. Barlow (1,735)
Staff: 1
33rd Massachusetts – Col. Adrian B. Underwood (498)
134th New York – Lt.Col. Allen H. Jackson (408)
136th New York – Col. James Wood Jr. (488)
73rd Ohio – Lt.Col. Richard Long Jr. (340)

ARTILLERY

I/1st New York Light Arty – Capt. Michael Weidrich (154) (6/3R)

3RD DIVISION

MG Carl Schurz (4,431)
Staff: 4

1ST BRIGADE

Brig.Gen. Alexander Schimmelfenning (1957)
Staff: 3
82nd Illinois – Lt.Col. Edward S. Solomon (471)
68th New York – Col. Gotthilf Von Bourry (284)
157th New York – Col. Phillip P. Brown (507)
61st Ohio – Col. Stephen J. McGrorty (307)

74th Pennsylvania – Lt.Col. Adolph von Hartung (385)

2ND BRIGADE

Col. Wladimir Krzyzanowski (1,518)
Staff: 3
58th New York – Lt.Col. August Otto (225)
119th New York – Col. Elios Peissner (382)
75th Pennsylvania – Col. Francis Mahler (267)
26th Wisconsin – Col. William H. Jacobs (641)

UNATTACHED

82nd Ohio – Col. James S. Robinson (484)

ARTILLERY

Staff: 1
I/1st Ohio Light Arty – Capt. Hubert Dilger (138) (6/12N)

RESERVE ARTILLERY

Lt.Col. Louis Schirmer (329)
Staff: 2
2nd Btty New York Light Arty – Capt. Hermann Jahn (114) (6/3R)
K/1st Ohio Light Arty – Capt. William L. DeBeck (113) (6/12N)
C/1st West Virginia Light Arty – Capt. Wallace Hill (100) (6/10P)

XII CORPS

Maj.Gen. Henry W. Slocum (12,796)
Staff: 8
Provost Guard 3 Cos./10th Maine – Capt. John D. Beardsley {176}

1ST DIVISION

Brig.Gen. Alpheus S. Williams (6,136)
Staff: 5

1ST BRIGADE

Brig.Gen. Joseph F. Knipe (1,749)
Staff: 1
5th Connecticut – Col. Warren W. Packer (284)
28th New York – Lt.Col. Elliott W. Cook (415)
46th Pennsylvania – Maj.Cyrus Strouss (361)
128th Pennsylvania – Col. Levi H. Smith (688)

2ND BRIGADE

Col. Samuel Ross (1,851)
Staff: 3
20th Connecticut – Lt.Col. William B. Wooster (490)
3rd Maryland – Lt.Col. Gilbert P. Robinson (375)
123rd New York – Lt.Col. James C. Rogers (643)
145th New York – Col. Edward L. Price (340)

3RD BRIGADE

Brig.Gen. Thomas H. Ruger (2,208)
Staff: 1
27th Indiana – Col. Silas Colgrove (489)
2nd Massachusetts – Col. Samuel M. Quincy (454)
13th New Jersey – Col. Ezra A. Carman (501)
107th New York – Col. Niram M. Crane (402)
3rd Wisconsin – Col. William Hawley (361)

ARTILLERY

Capt. Robert H. Fitzhugh (332)
Staff: 1
K/1st New York Light Arty – 1st Lt. Edward Bailey (104) (6/12N)

M/1st New York Light Arty – 1st Lt. Charles E. Winegar (112) (4/10P)
F/4th US Arty – Capt. Clermont L. Best/1st Lt. Crosby (105) (6/10P)

2ND DIVISION

Brig.Gen. John W. Geary (6,476)
Staff: 5

1ST BRIGADE

Col. Charles Candy (2,334)
Staff: 17
5th Ohio – Col. John H. Patrick (382)
7th Ohio – Col. William R. Creighton (381)
29th Ohio – Capt. Wilber F. Stevens (380)
66th Ohio – Col. Eugene Powell (376)
28th Pennsylvania – Maj.Lansford F. Chapman (406)
147th Pennsylvania – Lt.Col. Ario Pardee (392)

2ND BRIGADE

Brig.Gen. Thomas L. Kane (1,949)
Staff: 3
29th Pennsylvania – Lt.Col. William Richards Jr. (378)
109th Pennsylvania – Col. Henry J. Stainrook (171)
111th Pennsylvania – Col. George A. Cobham Jr. (217)
124th Pennsylvania – Lt.Col. Simon Litzenberg (636)
125th Pennsylvania – Col. Jacob Higgins (544)

3RD BRIGADE

Brig.Gen. George S. Greene (1,951)
Staff: 3
60th New York – Col. Abel Goddard (339)
78th New York – Lt.Col. Herbert Von Hammerstein (329)
102nd New York – Col. James Crandall (320)
137th New York – Col. David Ireland (477)
149th New York – Col. Henry A. Barnum (483)

ARTILLERY

Capt. Joseph M Knap (237)
Staff: 2
E/Pennsylvania Arty – 1st Lt. Charles A. Atwell (148) (6/10P)
F/Pennsylvania Arty – 1st Lt. Fleming {87} (4/3R)

CAVALRY CORPS

Brig.Gen. John Stoneman (10,626)
Staff: 25

1ST DIVISION

Brig.Gen. Alfred Pleasonton (3,437)
Staff: 11

1ST BRIGADE

Col. Benjamin F. Davis (1,970)
Staff: 4
8th Illinois – Maj. John L. Beveridge (472)
3rd Indiana – Col. George Henry Chapman (337)
8th New York – 1st Lt. Hermann Foerster (585)
9th New York – Col. Rush C. Hawkins (367)
3rd West Virginia – Capt. James Utt (205)

2ND BRIGADE

Col. Thomas C. Devin* (1,347)
Staff: 5
L/1st Michigan – 1st Lt. John C. Truax (75)
6th New York – Lt.Col. Duncan McVicar (293)
8th Pennsylvania – Maj. Pennock Huey (496)
17th Pennsylvania – Col. Josiah H. Kellogg (478)

ARTILLERY

6th (G) Btty/New York Light Arty – 1st Lt. Joseph Martin (109) (6/3R)

2ND DIVISION

Brig.Gen. William W. Averell (2,744)
Staff: 4

1ST BRIGADE

Col. Horace B. Sargent (1,555)
Staff: 19
1st Massachusetts – Lt.Col. Greely Stevenson Curtis (253)
4th New York – Col. Louis DiCesnola (298)
6th Ohio – Maj. Benjamin C. Stanhope (482)
1st Rhode Island – Lt.Col. John L. Thompson (503)

2ND BRIGADE

Col. John B. McIntosh (1,110)
Staff: 1
3rd Pennsylvania – Lt.Col. Edward S. Jones (394)
4th Pennsylvania – Lt.Col. William E. Doster (304)
16th Pennsylvania – Lt.Col. Lorenzo Rogers (411)

ARTILLERY

A/2nd US Arty – Capt. John C. Tidball (75) (6/3R)

3RD DIVISION

Brig.Gen. David McM. Gregg (4,420)
Staff: 4

1ST BRIGADE

Col. Judson Kilpatrick (1,150)
Staff: 1
1st Maine – Col. Calvin S. Donty (552)
2nd New York – Col. Judson Kilpatrick (264)
10th New York – Maj. Mathew H. Avery (333)

2ND BRIGADE

Col. Percy Wyndham (1,118)
Staff: 1
12th Illinois – Lt.Col. Hasbrouck Davis (268)
1st Maryland – Lt.Col. James M. Deems (295)
1st New Jersey – Lt.Col. Virgil Brodrick (199)
1st Pennsylvania – Col. John P. Taylor (355)

REGULAR RESERVE CAVALRY BRIGADE

Brig.Gen. John Buford (1,869)
Staff: 2
6th Pennsylvania – Maj.Robert Morris Jr. (244)
1st US Cavalry – Capt. R.S.C. Lord (380)
2nd US Cavalry – Maj.Charles J. Whiting (418)
5th US Cavalry – Capt. James E. Harrison (343)
6th US Cavalry – Capt. George C. Cram (482)

HORSE ARTILLERY

Capt. James M. Robertson (279)
Staff: 2

B&L/2nd US Arty – 1st Lt. Albert O. Vincent (99) (6/3R)
M/2nd US Arty – 1st Lt. Robert Clarke (117) (6/3R)
E/4th US Arty – 1st Lt. Samuel S. Elder (61) (4/3R)

*Not with Stoneman's Raid 29 April-7 May 1863

ARMY OF NORTHERN VIRGINIA

General Robert E. Lee
(62,682)

Chief Of Staff – Col. Robert H. Chilton
Chief Engineer – Col. W.P. Smith
ADC – Col. Marshall
Staff: 17

I CORPS

(Longstreet, Hood, Pickett, Dearing, Henry, in SE VA)
(18,504)

1ST DIVISION

Maj.Gen. Richard H. Anderson (8,673)
Staff: 7

MAHONE'S BRIGADE (1ST)

BF Wm. Mahone (1,797)
Staff: 4
6th Virginia – Col. Geo. T. Rogers (335)
12th Virginia – Lt.Col. Everard M. Field (434)
16th Virginia – Lt.Col. Richard O. Whitehead (307)
41st Virginia – Col. Wm. A. Parham (324)
61st Virginia – Col. Virginius D. Groner (393)

POSEY'S BRIGADE (2ND)

Brig.Gen. Carnot Posey (1,612)
Staff: 4
12th Mississippi – Lt.Col. Merry B. Harris (369)
16th Mississippi – Col. Samuel E. Baker (489)
19th Mississippi – Col. Nathaniel H. Harris (423)
48th Mississippi – Col. Joseph M. Jayne (327)

PERRY'S BRIGADE (3RD)

Brig.Gen. E.A. Perry (851)
Staff: 3
2nd Florida – Maj. Walton R. Moore (277)
5th Florida – Maj. Benjamin F. Davis (349)
8th Florida – Col. David Lang (222)

WILCOX'S BRIGADE (4TH)

Brig.Gen. C.M. Wilcox (2,261)
Staff: 5
8th Alabama – Col. Young L., Royston (533)
9th Alabama – Maj. Jeremiah Williams (419)
10th Alabama – Col. Wm. H. Forney (411)
11th Alabama – Col. John C.C. Sanders (426)
14th Alabama – Col. Lucius Pinckard (467)

WRIGHT'S BRIGADE (5TH)
Brig.Gen. A.R. Wright (1,709)
Staff: 4
3rd Georgia – Maj. John F. Jones (580)
22nd Georgia – Col. Joseph Wasden (459)
48th Georgia – Col. Wm. Gibson, Lt.Col. Reuben W. Carswell (467)
2nd Georgia Battalion – Maj. George W. Ross (199)

ARTILLERY
Lt.Col. John J. Garnett (436)
Staff: 9
Grandy's Virginia Btty (Norfolk Light Arty Blues) – Capt. Charles R. Grandy (110) (2/12N, 2-12H, 2-3R)
Lewis' Virginia Btty (Pittsylvania Btty) – Capt. Nathan Penick (96) (2/3R, 2/10P)
Maurin's Louisiana Btty (Donaldson Arty) – Capt. Victor H. Maurin (115) (2/10P, 1/3R, 3/6lb)
Moore's Virginia Btty (Norfolk Arty Aka Huger's) – Capt. Joseph D. Moore, (106) (1/3R, 1/10P, 2/6lb)

2ND DIVISION (MCLAW'S) DIVISION

Maj.Gen. Lafayette McLaws (9,831)
Staff: 4

KERSHAW'S BRIGADE (1ST)
Brig.Gen. Joseph B. Kershaw (2,349)
Staff: 6
2nd South Carolina (Palmetto) Regiment – Col. John D. Kennedy (412)
3rd South Carolina – Maj. Robert C. Maffett (415)
7th South Carolina – Col. Elbert Bland (409)
8th South Carolina – Col. John N. Henagen (300)
15th South Carolina – Lt.Col. Joseph F. Gist (526)
3rd South Carolina (Laurens) Battalion – Col. Wm. G. Rice (281)

SEMMES' BRIGADE (2ND)
Brig.Gen. Paul J. Semmes (1,957)
Staff: 4
10th Georgia – Lt.Col. Willis C. Holt (467)
50th Georgia – Lt.Col. Francis Kearse (442)
51st Georgia – Col. Wm. M. Slaughter (516)
53rd Georgia – Col. James P. Simms (528)

WOFFORD'S BRIGADE (3RD)
Brig.Gen. W.T. Wofford (1,954)
Staff: 4
16th Georgia – Col. Henry P. Thomas (439)
18th Georgia – Col. Solon Z. Ruff (408)
24th Georgia – Col. Robert McMillan (409)
Cobb's Georgia Legion – Lt.Col. Luther K. Glen (393)
Phillips' Georgia Legion – Lt.Col. E.S. Barclay Jr. (301)

BARKSDALE'S BRIGADE (4TH)
Brig.Gen. William Barksdale (2,212)
Staff: 4
13th Mississippi – Col. James W. Carter (551)
17th Mississippi – Col. Wm. D. Holder (608)
18th Mississippi – Col. Thomas M. Griffin (589)
21st Mississippi – Col. Benjamin G. Humphries (460)

ARTILLERY
Col. H.C. Cabell (406)
Staff: 4
Carlton's Georgia Btty (Troop Arty) – Capt. H. H. Carlton (101) (2/10P, 12H, 2/6lb)
1st Co., McCarthy's Virginia Btty (Richmond Howitzers) – Capt. Edward S. McCarthy (94) (2/10P, 2/6lb)
A/1st Regt. Manly's North Carolina Btty (Ellis Light Arty) – Capt. Basil C. Manly (139) (2/12H, 3/6lb)
Frasier's Pulaski (Georgia) Btty – (68) (2/3R, 2/10P)

ARTILLERY RESERVE (949)
Alexander's Battalion – Col. E.P. Alexander (581)
Staff: 9
Eubank's Virginia Btty (Bath Arty) – 1st Lt. Osmond B. Taylor (95) (4/12N)
Jordan's Virginia Btty (Bedford Light Arty) – Capt. Tyler C. Jordan (78) (4/3R)
Moody's Louisiana Btty (Madison Light Arty) – Capt. Geo. V. Moody (135) (2/3R, 2/24H)
Parker's (Richmond) Virginia Btty – Capt. Wm. W. Parker (90) (2/3R, 2/12H)
Rhett's South Carolina Btty (Brooks Light Arty) – Capt. A.B. Rhett (71) (2/20P, 2/10P)
Woolfolk's Virginia Btty (Ashland Arty) – Capt. Pichegru Woolfolk (103) (2/20P, 2/12N)

WASHINGTON LOUISIANA ARTILLERY
Col. James B. Walton (368)
Staff: 9
1st Company (Squire's) – Capt. C.W. Squires (107) (3/3R, 1/10P)
2nd Company (Richardson's) – Capt. John B. Richardson (80) (2/6N, 2/12H)
3rd Company (Miller's) – Capt. Merritt B. Miller (92) (2/12N)
4th Company (Eschelman's) – Capt. Benjamin H. Eschelman (80) (1/10P, 1/3R, 1/12N, 1/10P)

II CORPS

Lt.Gen. Thomas J. Jackson (39,870)
ADC – 1st Lt. James Power Smith
Staff: 15
Provost Guard, **1st Va. Irish Battalion** – Maj. David B. Bridgeford (123)

1ST DIVISION – HILL'S (LIGHT) DIVISION

Maj.Gen. A.P. Hill (11,442)
Staff: 12

HETH'S BRIGADE (1ST)
Brig.Gen. Henry Heth (1,283)
Staff: 4
40th Virginia – Col. J.M. Brockenborough (347)
47th Virginia – Col. Robert M. Mayo (262)
55th Virginia – Col. Francis Malory (388)
22nd Virginia Battalion – Col. Edwin P. Taylor (282)

PENDER'S BRIGADE (2ND)
Brig.Gen. W.D. Pender (1,796)
Staff: 4
13th North Carolina – Col. Alred M. Scales (448)

16th North Carolina – Col. John Smith McElroy (426)
22nd North Carolina – Lt.Col. Christopher C. Cole (441)
34th North Carolina – Col. William J. Lowrance (148)
38th North Carolina – Col. William J. Hoke (329)

MCGOWAN'S BRIGADE (3RD)
Brig.Gen. S. McGowan (2,216)
Staff: 4
1st South Carolina – Col. D.H. Hamilton (432)
12th South Carolina – Col. John L. Miller (368)
13th South Carolina – Col. Oliver E. Edwards (481)
14th South Carolina – Col. Abner M. Perrin (452)
1st Regt. South Carolina (Orr's) Rifles – Capt. James Monroe Perrin (479)

LANE'S BRIGADE (4TH)
Brig.Gen. James H. Lane (2644)
Staff: 4
7th North Carolina – Col. Edward G. Haywood (501)
18th North Carolina – Col. James T. Purdie* (500)
28th North Carolina – Col. Samuel D. Lowe (453)
33rd North Carolina – Col. Clarke M. Avery (569)
37th North Carolina – Col. Wm. M. Barbour (617)

ARCHER'S BRIGADE (5TH)
Brig.Gen. J.J. Archer (1,562)
Staff: 4
13th Alabama – Col. Birkett D. Fry (369)
5th Alabama Battalion – Capt. S.D. Stewart (197)
1st Regt. Provisional Tennessee – Lt.Col. Newton J. George (347)
7th Tennessee – Col. John A. Fite (389)
14th Tennessee – Col. Wm. McComb (256)

THOMAS'S BRIGADE (6TH)
Brig.Gen. E.L. Thomas (1,518)
Staff: 4
14th Georgia – Col. Robert W. Folsom (406)
35th Georgia – Capt. John Duke (369)
45th Georgia – Col. Washington L. Grice (372)
49th Georgia – Col. Samuel T. Player (367)

ARTILLERY
Col. R.L. Walker (411)
Staff: 4
Brunson's South Carolina Btty (Pee Dee Arty) – Capt. Ervin B. Brunson (70) (1/10P, 1/3R, 1/12N, 1/12H)
Crenshaw's Richmond Virginia Btty – 1st Lt. John H. Chamberlayne (82) (2/10P, 2/12H)
Davidson's Richmond Virginia Btty (Letcher Arty) – Capt. Greenlee Davidson (82) (2/6lb, 2/3R)
McGraw's (Purcell) Richmond Virginia Btty – Capt. William J. Pegram/1st Lt. Joseph McGraw (94) (4/12N)
Marye's Virginia Btty (Fredericksburg Arty) – Capt. Edward A. Marye (79) (12/2N, 2/10P)

2ND (RODES') DIVISION

Brig.Gen. R.E. Rodes (10,993)
Staff: 14

RODE'S BRIGADE (1ST)
Brig.Gen. R.E. Rodes/ Col. E.A. O'Neal (2,505)
Staff: 3
3rd Alabama – Capt. M.F. Bonham (509)

5th Alabama – Col. Josephus M. Hall (595)
6th Alabama – Col. James N. Lightfoot (544)
12th Alabama – Col. Samuel B. Pickens (419)
26th Alabama – Lt.Col. John S. Garvin (435)

DOLE'S BRIGADE (2ND)
Brig.Gen. Geo. Doles (1,760)
Staff: 4
4th Georgia – Col. Philip Cook (496)
12th Georgia – Col. Edward Willis (399)
21st Georgia – Col. John T. Mercer (376)
44th Georgia – Col. John B. Estes (485)

IVERSON'S BRIGADE (3RD)
Brig.Gen. Alfred Iverson (1,852)
Staff: 4
5th North Carolina – Col. Thomas M. Garvett (551)
12th North Carolina – Maj. David P. Rowe (338)
20th North Carolina – Col. Thomas F. Toon (472)
23rd North Carolina – Col. Daniel H. Christie (487)

COLQUITT'S BRIGADE (4TH)
Brig.Gen. Alfred H. Colquitt (2,623)
Staff: {4}
6th Georgia – Col. John T. Lofton {616}
19th Georgia – Col. Andrew J. Hutchins (367)
23rd Georgia – Col. Emory F. Best {649}
27th Georgia – Col. Charles T. Zachary {657}
28th Georgia – Col. Tully Graybill {330}

RAMSEUR'S BRIGADE (5TH)
Brig.Gen. S.D. Ramseur (1,815)
Staff: 4
2nd North Carolina – Col. Wm. R. Cox (502)
4th North Carolina – Col. Byran Grimes (456)
14th North Carolina – Col. Risden T. Bennett (449)
30th North Carolina – Col. Francis M. Parker (404)

ARTILLERY
Lt.Col. T.H. Carter (424)
Staff: 2
Reese's (Jefferson Davis) AL Btty – Capt. Wm. J. Reese (89) (2/3R, 2/12H)
Carter's Virginia Btty (King William Arty) – Capt. Wm. P. Carter (119) (1/10P, 2/12H, 2/6lb)
Fry's Virginia Btty (Orange Arty) – Capt. Charles W. Fry (90) (1/3R, 1/12H, 2/6lb)
Page's Virginia Btty (Morris Arty) – Capt. Richard C.M. Page (124) (2/3R, 1/12H, 3/6lb)

3RD (EARLY'S) DIVISION)
Maj.Gen. Jubal A. Early (8,284)
Staff: 12

GORDON'S BRIGADE (1ST)
Brig.Gen. John B. Gordon (2,045)
Staff: 6
13th Georgia – Col. James M. Smith (390)
26th Georgia – Col. Edmund N. Atkinson (339)
31st Georgia – Col. Clement A. Edmunds (278)
38th Georgia – Col. James D. Mathews (361)
60th Georgia – Col. Wm. H. Stiles (338)
61st Georgia – Col. John H. Lamar (333)

HOKE'S BRIGADE (2ND)
Brig.Gen. Robert F. Hoke (2,368)
Staff: 2
6th North Carolina – Col. Isaac M. Avery (576)
21st North Carolina – Col. William S. Rankin (567)
54th North Carolina – Col. James C.S. McDowell (679)
57th North Carolina – Col. Archibald C. Goodwin (430)
1st North Carolina Battalion Sharpshooters – Maj. Rufus W. Wharton (114)

SMITH'S BRIGADE (3RD)
Brig.Gen. Wm. Smith (1,532)
Staff: 4
13th Virginia – Lt.Col. James B. Terrill (325)
49th Virginia – Col. Jaonathan C. Gibson (298)
52nd Virginia – Col. Michael G. Harman (267)
58th Virginia – Col. Francis H. Board {638}

HAYS' BRIGADE (4TH)
Brig.Gen. Harry T. Hays (1,956)
Staff: 3
5th Louisiana – Col. Henry Forno (272)
6th Louisiana – Col. Wm. Monaghan (399)
7th Louisiana – Col. Davidson B. Penn (353)
8th Louisiana – Col. Trevanian D. Lewis (466)
9th Louisiana – Col. Leroy A. Stafford (463)

ARTILLERY
Lt.Col. S.R. Andrews (371)
Staff: 2
Brown's Maryland Btty (Chesapeake Battalion) – Capt. Wm. D. Brown (81) (2/10P, 2/3R)
Carpenter's Virginia Btty (Allegheny Roughs) – Capt. John C. Carpenter (95) (2/3R, 2/12H)
Dement's Maryland Btty//(1st Co. Maryland Flying Battery) – Capt. Wm. F. Dement (99) (4/6lb)
Raine's Virginia Btty (Lee Battery) – Capt. Charles I. Raine (94) (1/12H, 3/3R)

4TH (COLSTON'S) DIVISION
Brig.Gen. R.E. Colston (7,666)
Staff: 7

PAXTON'S BRIGADE (1ST)
Brig.Gen. E.F. Paxton (1,816)
Staff: 4
2nd Virginia – Col. John Quincy Adams Nadenbousch (399)
4th Virginia – Col. Wm. Terry (426)
5th Virginia – Col. J.H.S. Funk (470)
27th Virginia – Col. James K. Edmundson (221)
33rd Virginia – Lt.Col. Abraham Spengler (296)

JONES' BRIGADE (2ND)
Brig.Gen. J.R. Jones (1,671)
Staff: 7
21st Virginia – Maj. John S. Moseley (225)
42nd Virginia – Col. Robert W. Withers (400)
44th Virginia – Col. Norvell Cobb (304)
48th Virginia – Col. Thomas S. Garnett (377)
50th Virginia – Col. Alexander S. Vandeventer (358)

WARREN'S BRIGADE (3RD)
Col. E.T.H. Warren (2,625)
Staff: 5
1st North Carolina – Col. John A. MacDowell (576)

3rd North Carolina – Lt.Col. S.D. Thruston (780)
10th Virginia – Lt.Col. Samuel T. Walker (533)
23rd Virginia – Lt.Col. Simeon T. Walton (333)
37th Virginia – Col. Titus Vespasian Williams (398)

NICHOLL'S BRIGADE (4TH)
Brig.Gen. Francis T. Nicholls (1,547)
Staff: 3
1st Louisiana – Capt. Edward D. Willett (218)
2nd Louisiana – Col. Jesse M. Williams (362)
10th Louisiana – Lt.Col. John M. Legett (312)
14th Louisiana – Lt.Col. David Zable (362)
15th Louisiana – Lt.Col. William Michie (290)

ARTILLERY
Lt.Col. Hilary P. Jones (312)
Staff: 9
Carrington's Virginia Btty (Charlottesville Arty) – Capt. James M. Carrington (76) (4/6N)
Garber's Virginia Btty (Staunton Arty) – 1st Lt. Alexander H. Fultz (65) (4/6N)
Latimer's Virginia Btty (Courtney Arty) – Capt. W. A. Tanner (96) (4/3R)
Thompson's Btty (Louisiana Guard Artillery) – Capt. Charles Thompson (66) (2/10P, 2/3R)

GENERAL ARTILLERY RESERVE
Col. J. Thompson Brown (1,470)
Staff: 9
Brooke's (Warrenton) Virginia Btty – Capt. James B. Brooke (59) (2/12H, 2/6N)
Dance's Virginia Btty (Powhatan Arty) – Capt. Willis J. Dance (84) (1/3R, 1/6lb, 2/12H)
Graham's (Rockbridge) Artillery – Capt. Archibald Graham (93) (2/10P, 2/12H, 2/6lb)
Hupp's Virginia Btty (Salem Artillery) – Capt. Abraham Hupp (70) (2/12H, 2/6lb)
Smith's Btty (3rd Richmond Howitzers) – Capt. Benjamin H. Smith (64) (4/3R)
Watson's Btty (2nd Richmond Howitzers) – Capt. David Watson (66) (4/10P)

MCINTOSH'S BATTALION
Maj. David G. McIntosh (369)
Staff: 4
Hurt's (2nd Hardaway) Alabama Btty – Capt. William P. Hurt (75) (2/3R, 2/W)
Johnson's (Richmond) Virginia Btty – Capt. Marmaduke Johnson (100) (2/3R, 2/12H)
Lusk's (2nd Rockbridge) Virginia Btty – Capt. John A.M. Lusk (72) (2/3R, 2/12H)
Wooding's Virginia Btty (Danville Artillery) – Capt. Robert S. Rice (118) (2/10P, 1/3R, 1/12N)

RESERVE ARTILLERY
Brig.Gen. William N. Pendleton (656)
Staff: 3

CUTT'S (SUMTER GEORGIA) BATTALION
Lt.Col. A.S. Cutts (393)
Staff: 9
Ross's Btty (Sumter, A Btty) – Capt. Hugh M. Ross (130) (3/10P, 1/3NR, 1/12H, 1/12N)
Patterson's Btty (Sumter, B Btty) – Capt. George M. Patterson (130) (4/12H, 2/12N)
Wingfield's Btty (Sumter, C Arty) – Capt. John Wingfield (124) (3/NR, 2/10P)

NELSON'S BATTALION
Lt.Col. W. Nelson (260)
Staff: 9

Kirkpatrick's Virginia Btty (Amherst Artillery)
– Capt. Thomas J. Kirkpatrick (105) (2/12H, 2/6lb)

Massie's Virginia Btty (Fluvanna Arty) –
Capt. John L. Massie (73) (1/3R, 3/N)

Milledge's Georgia Btty – Capt. John Milledge
(73) (1/10P, 1/3R, 1/HR, 1/JR)

CAVALRY DIVISION

Maj.Gen. James E.B. Stuart (4,291)
Staff: 20
ADC – Maj. Heros von Borcke

FITZHUGH LEE'S BRIGADE (2ND)
Brig.Gen. Fitzhugh Lee (1,477)
Staff: 4

1st Virginia Cavalry – Col. James H. Drake
(311)

2nd Virginia Cavalry – Col. Thomas T. Munford
(387)

3rd Virginia Cavalry – Col. Thomas H. Owen
(225)

4th Virginia Cavalry – Col. Williams C.
Wickham (550)

WHF LEE'S BRIGADE (3RD)
Brig.Gen. W.H.F. (Rooney) Lee (2,131)
Staff: 4

2nd North Carolina Cavalry – Lt.Col. William
H. Payne (152)

5th Virginia Cavalry – Col. Thomas L. Rosser
(156)

9th Virginia Cavalry – Col. Rich L.T. Beale (494)

10th Virginia Cavalry – Col. James L. Davis
(241)

13th Virginia Cavalry – Col. John R. Chambliss
(305)

15th Virginia Cavalry – Col. Charles R. Collins
(779)

HORSE ARTILLERY
Maj. R.F. Beckham (663)
Staff: 9

Lynchburg (Beauregard) Rifles – Capt.
Marcellus N. Moorman (112) (4/6lb)

1st Stuart Horse Artillery – Capt. James
Breathed (107) (4/3R)

2nd Stuart Horse Artillery – Capt. Wiliam N.
McGregor (123) (2/12N, 2/3R)

Hart's South Carolina Artillery – Capt. James
F. Hart (107) (4/3R)

Ashby Virginia Arty – 1st Lt. Chew (99) (4/12N)

2nd Baltimore Light Arty – 1st Lt. W. Griffin
(106) (4/10P)

HOOKER'S BATTLE PLAN

Hooker's plan of attack at Chancellorsville was sound. Under Stoneman, Hooker sent 10,000 cavalrymen north and then west far above the Confederates to disrupt their supply lines; then they were to swing down and hit Lee from the flank or rear. Hooker sent General Sedgwick east with 59,000 men to feint at Fredericksburg, while he took 65,000 men across the Rappahannock at several fords to strike Lee's rear or flank. He wanted to create a diversion, or at least confusion, and then strike while the Confederates were trying to figure out where the real threat lay.

Hooker learned from Sharp that their moves telegraphed their strategy to Southern commanders. Lowe's two balloons might see and report Confederate actions, but Southern sympathizers everywhere were the additional eyes and ears of Lee's army, keeping him informed of Union movements despite the absence of Confederate cavalry. With every movement of Union troops, local citizens observed the direction and relative size of units and then reported every few hours via runners, slaves, and personal trips what the Union units were doing. Using confinement and restriction on personal movement, Hooker slapped a gag on Southern sympathizers. Moreover, he kept his own counsel, in much the same manner as Jackson is said to have done, telling his commanders only that which they immediately needed to know. If corps commanders knew little, brigade commanders knew less, and the men had scarcely any idea at all of Hooker's plans.

Whereas Jackson was somewhat more controlling and micromanaging, often giving instructions to his unit commanders of what route to take from one cross-roads to the next, Hooker was a bit more open with a handful of commanders as to his route of march. He enacted what today would be called a "need to know" policy. By limiting the amount of individuals who knew the plan of the campaign, Hooker limited the amount of men who knew the secret, and the fewer who knew, the fewer who could let it slip.

Hancock and French crossed at Banks Ford. Sickles, Reynolds, and Sedgwick were sent below Fredericksburg to hold the Confederate Army in place. Slocum and Howard crossed at Germanna Ford, and Meade crossed at Ely's Ford. All those fording the river met at a strategic crossroad where stood a solitary farmhouse: Chancellorsville. They now had to shift east to uncover Banks Ford which would help secure uncontested supply for both parts of the Army of the Potomac. As battles went, Hooker was winning, for the Army of the Potomac had the initiative, superior manpower, and the element of surprise.

Lee learned from Jackson of the Union crossing at Fredericksburg from the east, but because of the disposition of Union troops, he could not decide what Hooker's plan of attack was. Stuart's cavalry sent word of the Union cavalry's northern crossing and of Union troops moving south. Lee sent Anderson to hold the Chancellorsville junction of the Orange Plank and Mine roads near Zoan Church. He was short-handed, because Longstreet was away in Suffolk with Pickett and Hood's men.

Lee had about 58,000 men in total (his army was half the size of Hooker's) and he was certain that Hooker expected him to retreat; for that very reason, he was reluctant to do so. He met with Jackson to discuss their options. In a communique to Richmond, Lee stated, "It throws open a broad margin of our frontier, and renders our railroad communications more hazardous and more difficult to secure." He went on to say, "If I had Longstreet, [I] would feel safe."

CHANCELLORSVILLE: DAY ONE

Fightin' Joe Hooker was confident he would smash Lee. His observation balloons – Washington and Eagle – manned by Professor Lowe could see enemy troop movement; his telegraph and new military codes could get messages around faster than couriers, and Colonel Sharpe's Military Information Bureau supplied him with information that made him the most accurately informed commander of the Army of the Potomac to date. Abandoning wagons in favor of faster-moving mules, Hooker's supplies could easily keep up with his troops. Hooker kept Lee at Fredericksburg, mesmerized by the winter quarters of the Army of the Potomac. With the arrival of good weather, Hooker acted.

Hooker's plan was simple: steal a march on Lee. He would send his cavalry wide to cut Lee off, send a force downstream below Fredericksburg to make Lee think that was the real threat, and meanwhile move his army stealthily north, then march west to come down through the fords and close on Lee's rear. Part of II Corps encamped across from Fredericksburg in full view of the Confederate observers remained stationary, casting doubt as to what Hooker planned. Hooker's cavalry would arrive from the west to disrupt communications, slash supply lines, and maintain a threat to the Confederate Army and capital, while his troops savaged the Army of Northern Virginia.

Hooker split his infantry into halves. Under Hooker, V, XI, and XII Corps would cross north and west of Fredericksburg. Sedgwick took I, III, and VI Corps south of Fredericksburg and threatened to cross downstream, while part of II Corps acted as a stationary diversion east of Fredericksburg.

Hooker's plan possessed one element many other Union plans had not: security. Virtually every civilian nearby or on the line of march was under house arrest to keep them from informing Lee of his actions. He kept his full plan from his commanders, so only a handful of men knew the real scope of it, and no one, except possibly Couch or Butterfield, understood what Hooker really wanted to accomplish. What a man did not know, he could not let slip, Hooker reasoned, and he was determined to surprise Lee. If his plans failed, it would not be because someone had leaked his intentions to the Confederates.

Union opening moves

Stoneman's cavalry rode out on 13 April 1863, moving north and then cutting west. He felt no sense or urgency and did not wish to overtire his mounts in forcing a march or crossing; this proved to be his undoing.

Rains began the night of 14 April, and flood waters made fords impassable to

Professor T.S.C. Lowe was in charge of the Union balloon corps. His balloons were a great help, although many of his aerial reports were militarily non-specific; he reported "a great many men" instead of brigades, divisions, or corps.

These Union artillerymen were photographed on 3 May 1863 across the river from Fredericksburg, where they doubtlessly supported Sedgwick's attack that finally broke through Barksdale's defenses at Marye's Heights.

Stoneman until 28 April. His march stalled at Warrenton Junction, on the Orange and Alexandria railroad. Although the weather bears part of the blame, the lion's share goes to Stoneman, who was unsure of how to use his cavalry corps and moved cautiously forward lest he encounter Stuart. His caution was part of the undoing of Hooker's masterplan. Union infantry began marching on 27 April 1863, moving up-river according to plan, unaware of the slowness of Stoneman's column. Because most civilians were under house arrest, and because the Army of the Potomac was moving away from the Confederate positions, they made headway with little comment.

Hooker sent pickets of the 75th Ohio (XI Corps) ahead of the column. Lt.Col. Duncan McVicar, an impetuous and brave Scotsman, commanded the 6th NY cavalry which probed his proposed route of march. This was one of only four cavalry units Hooker retained from Stoneman's force.

In the late evening of 28 April and early morning of 29 April, V, XI, and XII Corps crossed the Rappahannock at Kelly's Ford. Light Confederate cavalry probes plagued them but did little to slow their advance. Howard and Slocum's corps moved to Germanna Ford on the Rapidan. Slocum's XII Corps left first, and an hour later Howard's XI Corps followed his route of march. They moved along the easternmost edge of the Spotsylvania Wilderness. The thick wood was a mixed blessing, for although the Wilderness slowed movement and made scouting ahead difficult, it also hid the advance of the Union Army from Lee's eyes. Hooker should have kept that in mind, realizing that it protected each army from observation by the other. They skirmished with Stuart's cavalry near Wilderness Tavern, but chased off the light Confederate probe, losing only a few stragglers and men taken prisoner by the Confederates.

However, one man taken prisoner was a Belgian observer attached to XI Corps. Stuart's aide, Heros von Borke, questioned him in French. The Belgian revealed no details, possibly because he knew none. However, he knew enough to guess that Hooker was advancing in force and would surprise the Southerners. His one comment was, "Gentlemen... make your escape as quickly as possible; if not,... capture... is a certainty." It was not much, but it was enough for Stuart to send messengers to Lee telling him XI Corps was south of the Rappahannock. He did not know its destination, but its presence set off an uneasy feeling. Later probes yielded V Corps and XII Corps prisoners, and Stuart began to realize the scope of Hooker's advance.

Meade's V Corps moved east and south, encountering only mild resistance from pickets stationed at Ely's Ford. Once across, and worried that more Confederates might be at Todd's and U.S. Fords, Meade detached Sykes to secure those while he continued toward Chancellorsville. Confederate generals Carnot Posey and William Mahone's men controlled U.S. Ford. When they learned of a general Union advance and of Sykes heading toward them, obviously intent on cutting them off, they withdrew, leaving a regiment to slow Sykes' advance. They established new positions – Mahone at Ely's Ford and Posey astraddle the Orange Turnpike – and sent Lee their locations.

So far, so good: Hooker had met no opposition. His plan called for all corps to converge on Chancellorsville on 30 April. At 1100 hours on 30 April Meade arrived without problem, decided there was little threat, and sent for Sykes to rejoin him.

That evening the other corps converged on the Chancellorsville crossroads six miles west of Fredericksburg. Hooker had successfully placed an army as large as Lee's at the Confederate commander's

BELOW **Because Stuart's cavalry often struck suddenly and burned bridges, Union commanders had to put guards on their pontoon bridges to ensure their lines of retreat stayed open.**

rear, and Lee was unaware of his peril. Uncharacteristically, Meade was demonstratively happy about their success and was clearly ready to continue his advance. Slocum informed him that Hooker had specifically ordered them to stop, consolidate, and form a defensive position around Chancellorsville. Meade's jubilation turned sour. What did Hooker plan?

Quickly establishing his headquarters at the Chancellor home, Hooker sought information on how Sedgwick's diversion was progressing. Sedgwick sent a dispatch saying that although Confederates were still visible to his front, they had allowed him to establish two pontoon bridges across the river with little resistance. Perhaps they remembered Burnside's dismal attack and were waiting for the Union forces to again smash themselves against the fortified Confederate positions. There seemed to be little activity on the southern side. Hooker took this to mean that his plan was working, so he ordered Sickles' III Corps to leave Sedgwick and march northwest, cross the river, and join him at Chancellorsville.

Excitement was running high in the Union ranks. "Hurrah for Old Joe!" soldiers cheered. So far, the campaign had gone without a hitch. Perhaps the end was near; perhaps Fightin' Joe had outfoxed the Gray Fox and was going to thrash Lee; maybe Chancellorsville would prove to be as big a turning point as Waterloo. Perhaps Hooker was another Wellington. Evidently Hooker's morale boosting, security, and planning, like Wellington's, had translated into efficiency and military success. Hooker's campaign was on schedule, at least as far as the infantry was concerned. The rank and file had not yet heard that Hooker had ordered them to cease advancing. Like racehorses long stabled and denied the right to gallop, the Army of the Potomac was eager to charge headlong into combat and take on the rebels.

Although magnificent for crossing where no fords or bridges were present, pontoon bridges were cumbersome affairs which had to be transported to the bridge sites by huge wagons; often their presence telegraphed a commander's intentions.

Two roads led west from Fredericksburg. At Chancellorsville, the Orange Turnpike went west past the Wilderness Church. The Plank Road followed the Orange Turnpike west for a couple of miles, then turned south at Salem Church, looping west to rejoin it at Chancellorsville, and then splitting again at Wilderness Church to move southwest. By holding Chancellorsville, Hooker controlled the Orange Turnpike and controlled the way Lee must withdraw. By allowing Sedgwick to press Lee, Hooker gave Lee two choices: stand and fight, or

Engineers had one of the toughest jobs in the army, erecting bridges and fortifications, often under heavy enemy fire. These veterans are from Co. B, US Engineers.

Solomon Meredith led the Iron Brigade of Midwesterners proudly at Chancellorsville. Two months later they would again bear the brunt of the fighting at the first day at Gettysburg.

Although an able and trusted commander, McLaws was unaccountably slow to react on 4 May, when with some urging he could have linked with Early to destroy Sedgwick.

withdraw. If Lee stood, he would find himself trapped with Sedgwick before him and Hooker behind. If Lee withdrew, he would have to move across the line held by the Army of the Potomac and then Hooker would fall on him like a ton of bricks! No doubt Hooker smiled to himself when he said, "I have Lee in one hand, and Richmond in the other."

Confederate dilemma

Lee was confused. Earlier Jackson had discovered Sedgwick's force erecting pontoon bridges south of Fredericksburg, and had informed Lee of their presence, but strangely, Sedgwick had not forced a strong advance, although he had more than enough men to do so. The Iron Brigade spearheaded the crossing. Their advance drove the 13th Georgia pickets and the 6th Louisiana relief pickets away from their rifle pits and back toward Confederate lines where Early waited. It appeared that his position was going to bear the brunt of the Union assault. Lee ordered Jackson's men to fall back to the heights in preparation for an assault. Lee's strategy was to let the enemy come to his entrenched army rather than oppose its crossing. Straddling a river was hard for any army, and straddling a river and having to maintain the path of retreat while trying to capture the heights held by entrenched Confederates was a much more difficult process. But Sedgwick had inexplicably stopped.

J.E.B. Stuart's cavalry had skirmished and captured prisoners from all corps. He sent Lee a message stating that he had reason to believe a sizable Union force was now on their side of the river and moving east.

Lee makes his reply

Suddenly the situation made sense to Lee. The threatened crossing at Fredericksburg was a diversion. That was why the Union troops had been less than fully aggressive. The large Union force Stuart had sighted was the real threat. Weighing his options, Lee sent word to Jefferson Davis, "Their intention... is to turn our left, and probably... our rear. Our condition... favours their operations."

Knowing that Hooker had a more sophisticated plan than Burnside's headlong assault, Lee scanned the map of the area and noted the peninsula of good fighting ground bordered by the river and the Wilderness. At the heart of this area lay the Chancellorsville crossroad. No doubt Hooker would occupy them and then move toward the Army of Northern Virginia.

Lee saw his peril. He ordered Anderson, who was guarding the fords north of Fredericksburg, to move his brigades west toward Chancellorsville to counter any Union movements east toward Fredericksburg. He was to reinforce Mahone and Posey's positions. When Anderson arrived at Chancellorsville, he decided to withdraw further to the east where the fighting ground was better than the heavy woods surrounding the Chancellor farmhouse.

Next, Lee told McLaws to move from Early's left flank below Fredericksburg and go to Anderson's support. That would leave Early facing the apparently sedentary Sedgwick. Then he ordered Stuart to rejoin the main Confederate Army with all due haste, lest the Union Army cut him off and with the Wilderness and Union troops combined, make it impossible for him to rejoin Lee. Not only was Lee concerned for Stuart, but Stuart's cavalry represented a considerable portion of his command; and they were his eyes and ears. He would need them to keep him informed of Hooker's moves so he could work out what the slippery Union commander had planned.

That night heavy rains returned. At 2100 hours on 29 April Anderson moved his men west, ignoring the driving rain. He both cursed and thanked the rain – it concealed his movements, but it slowed his progress. Sometime before dawn on 30 April he set up his battle line on a small ridge near Zoan Church, about two miles east of Chancellorsville. His left flank was across the unfinished railroad cut, and his right flank extended over the Orange Turnpike. The rain lessened. Anderson's approach had been silent, and he held the high ground. Now all he could do was wait for dawn.

The officers of the 1st New York light artillery are shown gathered here, but in the battle of Chancellorsville their batteries were attached to several different commands.

These men of the 10th New York cavalry served under Judson Kilpatrick at Chancellorsville. They wear the varied uniforms of seasoned campaigners.

That night Lt.Col. Duncan McVicar's 6th New York Cavalry was moving west when they ran into Stuart's command of Virginia cavalry on the same road moving east. They met on the road to the Spotsylvania Court House, near the Henry Alsop house. Stuart's outriders were fired upon and rode back telling him they were under attack by Yankees. Prussian aide-de-camp Hero Von Borke rode ahead to investigate. Moments later he came flying back, crouched low over his horse's neck, firing his pistol into the darkness behind. Stuart beat a hasty retreat to Todd's Tavern, where he could gather his thoughts and document the enemy's strength and movements. Stuart ordered Fitzhugh Lee to find out how many Yankees were on the road. Lee sent the 5th Virginia as outriders and followed with his whole brigade.

After the brush with Confederate cavalry, McVicar knew trouble was coming, and his unit was not strong enough to fight stirrup to stirrup action. Dismounting his men, he formed skirmish lines in Alsop's field which was surrounded by a fence and accessible only through a gate. The 6th New York waited facing the gate. In the dark, the 5th Virginia entered Alsop's gate in a column of fours. Carbine fire slammed into them stopping them as they entered. Leaving the dead and dying, they withdrew. Stuart ordered more men forward but they were also stalled at the gate by Yankee small arms fire.

McVicar realized he was badly outnumbered and more Confederates were arriving all the time. If he stayed, his command would be annihilated. He mounted his men, drew his saber, and charged the disarrayed Southerners, intent on forcing his way through and back to his own lines. The Confederates had rallied somewhat, and were pushing toward the opening. Von Borke saw the 6th NY charge the gate. Confederate and Union cavalry collided in a crash of horseflesh and steel. While leading the charge, McVicar fell with a pistol ball through his heart. The Union survivors broke through.

Stuart hurled the 2nd Virginia cavalry at the Union troopers, splitting the Union command. Many were captured; some escaped; and many died. But their efforts slowed up the spectacular J.E.B. Stuart and kept him from immediately joining Lee a few miles away.

At dawn on 1 May Lee and Jackson surveyed the Federals across the river. Lee went over despatches, trying to fathom Hooker's plan, and then eyed Sedgwick's barely active troops. When the attack came, it would not be from these men. He told Jackson, "The... attack will come from above," meaning from the troops which were camped at Chancellorsville. Lee wired Jefferson Davis, informing him of what he supposed Hooker's plans were. "If I had Longstreet's division," he wrote, "[I] would feel safe." As it was, Lee was a gambler, and he decided to take a calculated risk. No doubt Hooker expected him to retreat when faced with attack from across the river, and then be surprised by the sudden appearance of Union troops along the Orange and Plank roads to the west. Retreat was possible, but it was not the option Lee would choose. Besides, he had a plan he wanted to discuss with Jackson. If his plan failed, he could still retreat.

Lee's idea was audacious: split his army. Leave a few men at Fredericksburg – a token army delaying a token army – and have a few hold an east-west line, then let Jackson take the remainder to strike the enemy. Lee wrote, "Leave sufficient troops to hold our lines, and with the main body... give battle to the approaching

This bridge was endangered by men marching to the tune of the band: their cadenced footfalls almost shook the bridge apart, and the band had to stop playing lest the bridge collapse.

Ambrose Wright was a Georgia lawyer turned soldier whose unit distinguished itself throughout the war. A reliable commander, he was instrumental in saving Jackson's artillery and stopping Sickles' men from advancing.

column." He continued, "At midnight on the 30th, General McLaws marched... toward Chancellorsville. Jackson followed at dawn next morning with the remaining divisions." His foot cavalry was on the move.

The Federal Army was tugging at its leash, anxious to close with what they believed to be an unsuspecting Southern Army. Hooker's intelligence told him Confederates had taken up position across the road to his east, but they were not there in strength, just a division, he imagined, unaware of McLaws' advance to reinforce Anderson, Posey, and Mahone.

Stonewall Jackson was up early on the morning of 1 May. Feeling that the day was something special, he donned his new uniform. He had worn it once before, when his wife had visited and had insisted he sit for a photograph. Gone was the crumpled old VMI kepi and the mud-stained and well-worn trousers and coat. Facing his reflection, Jackson saw a high-ranking Confederate general, resplendent and authoritative. At daybreak he rode past the 2nd North Carolina, hat in hand. "Stonewall's coming!" ran word along the lines of gray-clad troops approaching the Union Army. The thought made them stand straighter, march faster, and bear their weariness better. They arrived at the Orange Turnpike and Orange Plank Road positions about 0800 hours. Their Union counterparts were not aware that Jackson was coming, but they would know all too well when he arrived.

Lee's daring strategy

At dawn on 1 May Hooker thought Jackson still sat on the heights above Sedgwick. Lowe's 0900 report stated, "Heavy columns of the enemy's infantry and artillery are now moving up the river... a heavy reserve on the heights opposite the... crossing." Not a specific report; not even anything to cause Hooker worry; he expected the Confederates to reinforce their positions.

The sun rose and the day began to heat up. As far as the Union forces knew, only Anderson faced them. Hooker delayed several hours after dawn before he gave orders to advance. Sykes was to move down the Orange Turnpike and XII Corps down the Orange Plank Road. Howard's XI Corps was left in position at Wilderness Church. Hooker ordered Gibbon's II Corps to cross the river at Banks Ford.

Gibbon had problems. Many of his troops in Sully's division were due to muster out, and some felt their terms of enlistment dated from the day they signed on and not the day the government accepted their unit into service. Mutinous feelings were rampant among these short-time, two-year men. Earlier, Sully had not been able to convince his mutineers to cross and fight. Gibbon ordered his loyal soldiers to load weapons and face the mutineers, and then commanded the mutineers to return to their duties. No one moved. He readied the loyal troops and called out to the mutineers, "Every man who is ready to do his duty, step forward!" The unit hesitated, then cheered and moved forward. "Go... do your duty," Gibbon commanded. These soldiers crossed the river with Gibbon.

Lee told Jackson to "repulse the enemy." When Jackson arrived at the Confederate positions, he found McLaws' men entrenching. This was not what he planned. The Union knew there were Confederates here. What military value was there in this? He stopped the entrenching and ordered McLaws to move down the Orange Turnpike toward Chancellorsville. Mahone would lead, followed by McLaws, and with Perry and Wilcox's brigades guarding the rear of the line of march. Jackson would move up the Orange Plank Road. Wright and Posey's men would lead, followed by Hill and Rodes' divisions. Colston was still en route from below Fredericksburg and would provide reserves. By 1100 Jackson had rewritten the scenario from one of passively awaiting the Union advance to actively moving west to meet it.

At 1130 hours Sykes' lead elements came under fire from McLaws' Confederates spread across the Orange Turnpike. When Sykes ran into McLaws, he formed a line, with Slocum on his right and Hancock reinforcing him. Mahone's 12th Virginia skirmishers hit the 8th Pennsylvania cavalry, who gave way. Soon the cavalry was sandwiched between Confederate skirmishers in front and Union skirmishers behind. The Virginians forced Sykes back. Sykes gave ground grudgingly and sent Hooker word of stiffer-than-expected resistance.

Sykes found himself in advance of the Union line and beleaguered. On a low ridge, Mahone's Southern skirmishers formed behind a rail fence and poured

CAVALRY SKIRMISH

J.E.B. Stuart was trying to locate General Lee. With his staff he rode on what he thought were somewhat "safe" roads that evening. hearing something ahead, he sent Von Bourke to take a look. Soon afterwards the Prussian came galloping back followed by Union troopers in hot pursuit. Stuart and his staff put spurs to their mounts and rode away in the darkness toward the main body of Confederate cavalry.

Wilcox made every effort to reach Fredericksburg before Sedgwick broke Barksdale's line. As it was, his rearguard action delayed Sedgwick from joining Hooker and contributed greatly to Lee's victory.

rifle fire into the Yankees. After a brief firefight, the Federals rallied and charged the 12th Virginia. The Virginians were given the order to pull back but Capt. Banks of the 12th Virginia was dead; the 12th stood until a lieutenant took it upon himself to give the order to fall back. In the confusion, over 80 Southerners were captured. Soon Wright flanked Slocum, but failed to dislodge him, while Anderson's men attacked Sykes in front and on both flanks and McLaws assailed his left. A.P. Hill was not far behind the Confederate advance. Hancock moved forward to relieve Sykes' battered command. Meade's V Corps, still acting according to Hooker's original plan, encountered no resistance on the River Road and was within sight of Banks Ford by 1300 hours.

The battle on the Orange Turnpike ebbed and flowed until Semmes' Confederates joined the fray to turn the tide, forcing the Union troops back toward Chancellorsville.

Meanwhile Posey and Wright formed across the Plank Road after forcing their way through Union soldiers on the road to Catherine Furnace below Chancellorsville. The Confederates slogged through rapidly increasing marsh until Union artillery began slamming into the muddy fields around them. Stuart sent Jackson word that he was approaching his left flank. "I will close... and help all I can," Stuart wrote. Jackson scribbled a reply on Stuart's note, telling him, "Keep close on Chancellorsville."

Hooker vacillates

Resistance on the Orange Turnpike unnerved Hooker. His scenario called for a Confederate retreat, not an advance. He then made the decision which cost him the battle: he ordered all units to resume their original positions, giving up hard-earned ground which many Union commanders felt could have been held. At 1300 hours Hooker ordered Sykes to resume his position of the prior evening and connect with Slocum, building breastworks and digging trenches. Hooker then added, "General Couch will then retire to his position of last night."

Union commanders were flabbergasted. General Couch reported, "The position... abandoned was high ground... open in front, over which an army might move and artillery be used advantageously." Meade was more to the point, saying, "If he can't hold the top of the hill, how does he expect to hold the bottom of it?" Thus began Hooker's defeat.

By the end of the day the Army of the Potomac had more or less resumed its original position from that morning. This thicket-choked countryside spread out briefly at the crossroads. West of Chancellorsville lay the northern branch of the thick and dark Spotsylvania Wilderness. To the north lay the rivers; to the east, Fredericksburg. To the east and south Confederates pressed west and northwest respectively. Nothing had really changed since the morning, or had it?

Hooker's army felt secure, but unhappy. Meade's V Corps held the left flank, anchored at the Rappahannock and stretching south-southwest, just west of Mineral Springs Run. Couch's II Corps faced east, stretched between Meade's right flank and the junction of the Orange Turnpike and Orange Plank Road at Chancellorsville. South of Couch, Slocum's XII Corps faced south with its left flank butting against the Orange Turnpike, extending southwest over the Plank Road, and then swinging north to touch the Orange Turnpike again about three-quarters of a mile west of the Chancellor farmhouse. Situated along the Orange Turnpike west, Howard's XI Corps stretched over an area of two miles. XI Corps occupied the northern side of the pike, from half a mile west of Talley's Farm, east, moving to within a mile and a quarter west of Chancellorsville. With thick woods before, behind, and beside him to the west, Howard felt secure.

Unfortunately the thick woods concealed many paths and rural roads known only to locals, many partly overgrown and used only for logging, or poorly used as most of the traffic was on either the Turnpike or Plank Road. A little over a mile west of Howard's right flank the Brock Road met the Turnpike just east of Wilderness Tavern. It angled south-southeast below Confederate lines. As with many roads, this was not unmarked, just rarely used, but not so unused that a Confederate sympathizer did not know about it.

Lee wanted to act now that he knew what Hooker planned. Jackson took the imperative when he brought the battle to the Union troops on both the Orange Turnpike and the Orange Plank Road. Hooker gave up the initiative at the slightest show of Confederate resistance. Jackson's advance had swayed the tide of events to stop the Union advance. The next day Union leaders would learn that having their advance stopped was nothing compared to what was to come.

As evening approached, Stuart met with Lee. Lee was confused by the Army of the Potomac's recent actions. Slocum had been under attack from Wright, so his retreat made sense; however, Meade had also withdrawn, and he had not been under attack. The Army of the Potomac was in a natural redoubt formed of thickets, heavy woods and deadfalls now arranged as a defensive position. He made a short reconnaissance ride, but as night was falling and fog returning, he realized how dangerous it could be beyond the lines, so he returned to his headquarters puzzled over Hooker's possible plans for the next day.

Jackson was waiting for Lee's return. The camp was a hasty, ramshackled affair, and they employed discarded Union cracker crates as tables and chairs, studying the map by firelight in the gathering gloom.

Men like Hancock were the backbone of the Federal officer's corps. He steadfastly did his job and held positions assigned him. Without his help at Chancellorsville, Couch would have had a difficult time escaping Early.

Couch hoped to replace the shaken Hooker, who had been stunned by an artillery shell. Instead he was merely called to Hooker's side to relay messages to commanders; Hooker refused to turn over command.

Lt. Genl. T. J. Jackson & Staff

W. J. Hawks Maj. Chf. C.S.

R. L. Dabney Maj. A. A. G.

J. Hotchkiss Capt. Top. Engr.

W. Allan Lt. Col. Chf. Ord.

Hunter McGuire Maj. & Med. Dir.

A. S. Pendleton Lt. Col. A. A. G.

J. P. Smith Capt. A.D.C.

J. G. Morrison Capt. A.D.C.

H. K. Douglas Half.

D. B. Bridgeford Maj. P.M.

COPY RIGHT SECURED
Richmond Va.

In this compilation of Stonewall Jackson and staff, many of the men here were with Jackson at Chancellorsville the night he was wounded by friendly fire from Confederate pickets. Pendleton is to Jackson's immediate right.

45

Because of Sedgwick's apparent feint, Jackson felt that Hooker's probe was also a feint. Regardless, the Union advance had stalled, and now the Southerners could have the imperative if they wanted it. General Stuart arrived bearing a report from Fitzhugh Lee which stated the Army of the Potomac's position extended beyond Wilderness Church to the west and along the north edge of the Orange Turnpike. That was the bad news. The good news was that the Union Army had only woods on its right flank, and because they must have felt protected, they did not have any real fortifications or defenses on that flank. Howard's XI Corps held that flank and had few pickets out. Jackson studied the map, and proposed a plan. Lee listened, and then nodded.

Jackson's audacious plan

The plan was bold: Jackson was to take his entire corps, go west, and then cut north to attack the unprotected XI Corps, thus rolling up Hooker's line and leaving the Union Army disorganized. He would take roughly 28,000 troops plus Stuart's men, who would screen their advance, and leave Lee with only Anderson and McLaws' divisions facing the Union Army and holding it in position. Lee would feint and feign attacks as Sedgwick had done; his sleight of hand would allow Jackson to steal a march on Hooker.

Jackson faced many obstacles, but his faith in his foot cavalry was strong. He would move a dozen or more miles west across the front of the Union position, and then north. It was a tremendously risky maneuver. Lee wrote Jefferson Davis, "If the enemy is too strong for me... I shall... fall back. If successful here, Fredericksburg will be saved. I may be forced... to the Orange and Alexandria or Virginia Central... but... I will be in position to contest the enemy's advance." The object of Jackson's march and Lee's holding action against Hooker was to allow Jackson to "come up in his rear."

Lee later reported that they decided to "endeavor to turn his [Hooker's] right flank and gain his rear, leaving a force in front to hold him in check and conceal the movement." This was not greatly different from the plan Hooker had used in his attempt to destroy Lee. Conservatively, Lee decided Hooker's force numbered in excess of 45,000 men, and Sedgwick still had 30,000 troops facing Fredericksburg.

Dawn reddened the horizon as the meeting broke up. Jackson and Stuart hurried away to ready their commands for the move. Lee made certain McLaws and Anderson's men were ready for their part in the Confederate diversion. It would have been better if Jackson had had the protective cover of night to mask his approach, but the Army of Northern Virginia did not have that luxury. Tonight they would either have turned the Union right, or they would be withdrawing toward the railroads. Either way, Joe Hooker was in for a fight.

JACKSON & LEE CONFER

In the early hours of the morning of 1 May Jackson and Lee formulated the audacious march in front of the Union Army to flank it. Although the elements of the final plan were similar to the original, Jackson located a closer and more concealed route and so modified the original plan whilst on the march.

DAY TWO

Jackson mulled over the plan. Although a risk-taker, he did not needlessly expose his command to danger. The original route of march he proposed passed very close to Union lines. Was there a better way? His chaplain, B.T. Lacy, was from this area and Jackson called on him for advice: Did Lacy know a better way? Lacy did not, but he knew someone who would know if a better way existed – Charles C. Welford, manager of the Catharine Furnace. Jackson sent Lacy, accompanied by his chief engineer, Jed Hotchkiss, to find Welford.

Welford was glad to oblige. Not only did he know a shorter route than via Todd's Tavern, but it was a new wood cutter's road. Furthermore, he knew of another side road that was little used and should avoid enemy pickets. Now Jackson had a more concealed and faster route than originally planned. His eyes glinted bright blue in the early morning firelight.

Jackson took the revisions to Lee. Hotchkiss relates that Lee asked Jackson what he intended to do. Jackson's finger traced Welford's route on the map – "I propose to go right around there." Lee studied the route – "Go ahead."

Jackson sets out

At 0400 hours Jackson's bold trek began. Rodes led the column, followed by Colston, A.P. Hill, Archer, Thomas, and finally the artillery with the 23rd Georgia infantry acting as rear guard. It was warm, and the woods were filled with fog, which slowly burned off as the sun rose. Jackson's 28,000 troops marched slightly south, then west, and finally north to bring them behind the Union's right flank. Despite the early hour, they had a great distance to go, and to fully exploit the advantage they expected to gain, they should have started shortly after midnight. They were running late.

Lee's 15,000 men waited to Hooker's front. They could not be passive, for this would encourage a Union probe and could reveal their lack of strength. They could not conduct a real attack in strength either, for that, too, would reveal their weakness. All they could do was probe and feint attacks to keep Hooker guessing. The longer they could do this, the more time they would buy for Jackson.

Lee knew that reinforcements had strengthened the Union's left flank. Good: so far they had not guessed his plan. He told McLaws and Anderson what their role was, and that they should press the Federal left forcefully, but he reminded them that they were not to attack as more than a forceful probe "unless a favorable opportunity should present itself."

At 0730 hours Jackson's lead elements on the Orange Plank Road executed a left face and moved down a side road by Decker's Farm and the Catharine Furnace. Their route of march was a mile south of the Army of the Potomac, and moving west. Despite the earlier rain and morning fog, the day threatened to be sweltering, drying trees and deadfalls and making the dust rise where Southern feet tramped along the dirt roads.

Averell led a successful raid against Stuart after Fitzhugh Lee left him a taunting message. His action led to further Confederate raids, and Hooker vented his ire at Stoneman on the unfortunate Averell, who remained with Hooker's force.

Hooker takes stock

Hooker felt secure because his army was consolidated, his artillery was formed, and although Lee was not yet acting predictably, he was facing threats on two fronts. Hooker's cavalry was not present, but otherwise his plan was unfolding as foreseen. No doubt when Lee realized the situation, he would retreat. At the Bullock Farm, a large flat area just south of Mineral Springs Road and Ely's Ford Road, Hooker formed a reserve artillery park. He ordered Averell's cavalry forward to reconnoiter, and his weakest corps, Howard's XI Corps, was far west on the Union right, well away from any projected conflict.

The smallest corps, XI had possessed questionable morale since Sigel, a German, had left and Howard had assumed command. The motto of its mostly German troops was, "I fights mit Sigel." Hooker knew Howard had performed well at Manassas, but he knew his men were unhappy. To secure his right flank, Hooker ordered Reynolds to bolster Howard, but Reynolds probably could not be in position before dinner mess call.

First thing that morning Hooker inspected V and XII Corps' positions. These veterans of the peninsula and Antietam knew Southern capabilities and had prepared rifle pits, abatis, and breastworks. Meade, Hancock, and Couch knew it was better to be safe than sorry.

While Jackson was marching in front of the Union Army to surprise Hooker, Sickles set up a review of his troops for Hooker. After the review, Hooker visited Howard's XI Corps and asked Howard to strengthen his defenses.

At 0800 hours Hooker inspected Howard's position; both Sickles of III Corps and Capt. Cyrus Comstock (chief engineer of the Army of the Potomac) accompanied him. Howard joined them upon their arrival. He indicated his troop deployment, and noted that his greatly extended line had gaps between Devens and Schurz's divisions. Hooker was not unduly concerned, because according to his plan, XI Corps would be as far away from the potential action as any Union infantry on this side of the Rappahannock. Not only was XI Corps extended, but it was obvious to Comstock that Howard had not insisted on breastworks or defensive fortifications.

When Comstock studied XI Corps' disposition, he pulled Howard aside and suggested that he "close those spaces." The woods were thick, preventing freedom of any enemy movement, Howard felt. However, it also prevented accurate observation by his men – as any astute observer might have noted.

Howard's right flank had three units at a right angle to the Orange Turnpike: Dieckmann's 13th NY battery was supported by the 54th NY and 153rd PA infantry facing west, barely 700 men in all. The other units faced south. Howard showed Comstock how thick and impenetrable the Wilderness was, and implied that he felt safe from attack, asking, "Will anybody come through there?" Captain

JACKSON'S FLANKING MARCH, 2 MAY 1863

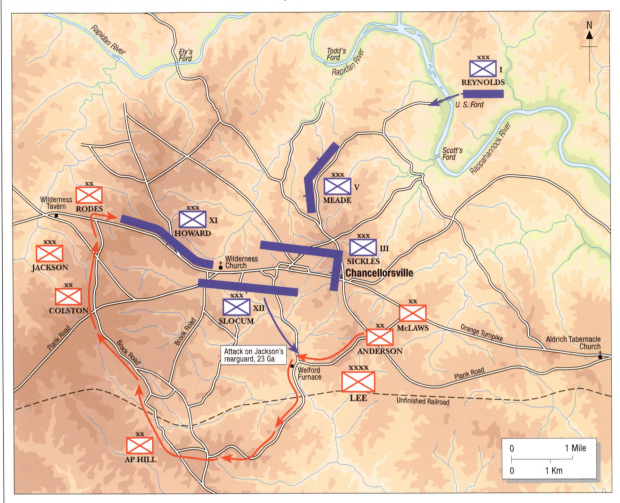

When Lee realized that Hooker had stolen a march on him and that he was hemmed in by Hooker to the north, Sedgwick to the east-southeast, and (potentially) Stoneman to the west, he decided that only Hooker was a real threat. Together he and Jackson planned an aggressive surprise for Hooker. Leaving Early to hold Sedgwick at Fredericksburg, Lee retained a few units to hold flimsy positions against the Union thrust on the Orange Turnpike while Jackson found a way to strike at Hooker's flanks and rear.

Comstock studied the woods and replied, "They may." But this observation appeared lost on Howard.

At 0900 hours Hooker returned to his command post at Chancellorsville and was greeted by Meade's message that his corps was under attack from the southeast. At the same time, Union observers reported seeing a sizable Confederate force to Sickles' front near Catharine Furnace, moving west. Hooker felt the Confederates were now withdrawing toward Gordonsville. That they were instead attempting a flanking movement did not seem likely to him, but he notified Howard so he would be aware of the enemy movements all the same and to make the necessary precautions

Hooker's message to Howard asked him to consider what he could do in case of a flank attack, and to "determine... the positions you will take... in whatever direction he advances." He told Howard to "have heavy reserves... to meet this contingency. The right of your line does not appear strong enough." The message concluded, "Advance your pickets for... observation... to obtain timely information of their approach."

Howard did not feel endangered. This was not an order, but a suggestion or conditional question. He felt the woods were defense enough, and that any attack would come from the south. Still, he replied to Hooker, writing, "I am taking measures to resist any attack from the west." With that, he ordered a rifle pit dug across the Chancellorsville Road at the rear of Schurz's division, near Dowdall's Tavern.

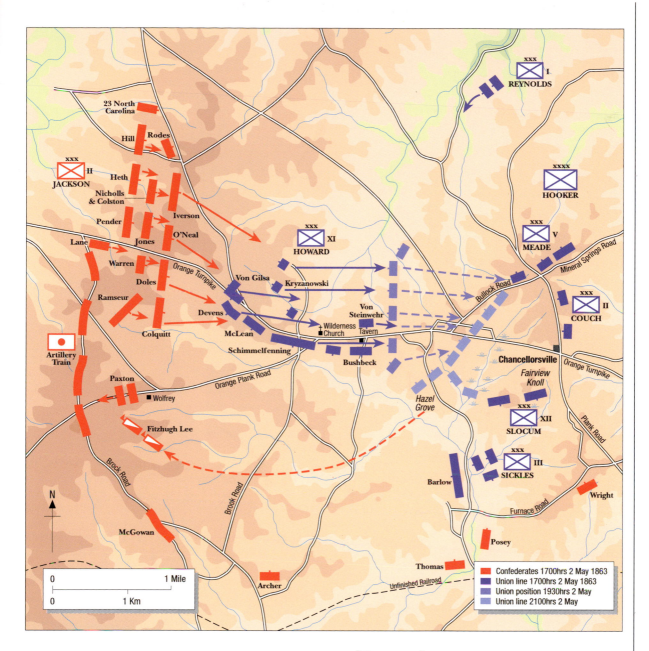

Confederates 1700hrs 2 May 1863
Union line 1700hrs 2 May 1863
Union position 1930hrs 2 May
Union line 2100hrs 2 May

Stonewall Jackson's corps was now in position west of the Army of the Potomac. Unknown to Howard, a Southern guide had located a logging road that took Jackson to XI Corps' flank. The Confederate charge overran many of XI Corps' campsites, routing Union troops. The speed of the Confederate advance, while it folded many Union defenses, also worked with nightfall against the Southerners, whose units became entangled – and they lost their cohesiveness.

Birney advances

At 1100 hours Devens reported heavy enemy presence passing by his front. Hooker weighed the alternatives: a Confederate attack, or a Confederate withdrawal? No reports of serious attacks arrived, and Hooker evidently decided that no real attack was forthcoming, and that the Confederates were withdrawing as he had planned. At 1300 Hooker ordered Sickles to "harass the movement" of the Confederates. Not attack, but harass.

At 1400 hours Hooker told Couch, "Lee is in full retreat, and I have sent Sickles out to capture his artillery." Later Hooker ordered Slocum to swing his men south in support of Sickles' move toward Catharine Furnace road. Slocum obeyed. This put Hazel Grove at Sickles and Slocum's rears.

Sickles' response to Hooker's order was to send Birney forward. At 1430 Birney's men hit the 23rd Georgia at Catharine Furnace. His attack killed or captured most of the Confederates. The 8th PA cavalry took part in the attack and in rounding up prisoners. One old horse-soldier commiserated with a Confederate veteran on how sorry it was to have been sacrificed so the main body could get away. The Rebel studied him and then answered defiantly, "You have done a big thing just now, but wait till Jackson gets round on your right." The cavalryman felt this statement of fact was bravado and ignored the comment.

Meanwhile, Jackson had been observing the unready appearance of XI Corps' troop dispositions. He ordered Rodes to advance and halt the head of the column at Dowdall's Tavern (Wilderness Tavern) on the south side of the Old Orange Turnpike, a mile west of the Union lines. At 1430 hours Rodes began

forming his men north of the Orange Turnpike. The 5th Alabama was west of XI Corps. Union pickets alerted commanders of Confederate activity, and they in turn reported to their commanders or Howard, but Howard did not act. He felt the Confederates were retreating as Hooker had said they would, and that the reports were "the offspring of... fears."

Hooker sent Sedgwick a telegram confirming his earlier supposition that Lee must either fight or flee, saying, "The enemy is fleeing, trying to save his trains." As far as Hooker knew, everything was going as planned.

When Lee learned of Birney's attack on Jackson's rear guard, he sent Posey to reinforce Wright on his left flank. The appearance of Posey's men halted Birney and made Sickles consolidate his forces because of Hooker's earlier directive to "harass." Unless strongly reinforced, Sickles would not advance against an undetermined enemy force. Hooker ordered Barlow of XI Corps (Howard's reserves) to move east and support Sickles. Instead of alerting Howard to a potentially dangerous situation, this movement seemed to convince him that XI Corps was in no danger.

Lull before the storm

By 1700 that evening Jackson's men were in position far to the Union right of where Howard's XI Corps had lit their supper campfires. The evening sun was behind Jackson and would be in his enemy's eyes when he attacked. He deployed his divisions carefully along the turnpike: Rodes, followed by Colston, with A.P. Hill in the rear. Stuart's cavalry and the Stonewall brigade were to stick to the road and hold the Southern right flank. Colquitt, adjacent to Stuart, was told his flank was secure, and to ignore anything happening there, and not let it interfere with his advance, as his flank was protected.

Jackson rode to the head of the column, aware of the eager eyes of the soldiers he passed. He moved alongside Rodes, saying, "You can go forward, sir." Rodes' division started east at a fast walk, rifles at low port, ready.

It was suppertime in the Union camp. Some troops were relaxing on their bedrolls, their muskets stacked, chatting with their messmates. These German-speaking troops had an imperfect command of English; they were comfortably seated around fires when the low howl of the rebel yell came from out of the sunset behind them.

From the trees to their west in the gathering gloom came an unearthly moan as ghostly gray shapes flitted toward them from the treeline. Musketry ripped into them. The Confederates changed from a fast walk to a charge, their weapons held higher, eyes hard, screaming a rebel yell. The Union soldiers were stunned. Before they could form a defensive position, indeed before many could grab weapons, Jackson's foot cavalry was among them.

Von Gilsa's 54th NY and 153rd PA faced the Confederate charge, firing into the oncoming Southerners. The 41st and 45th NY were totally surprised by the flanking movement. They broke and ran without fighting as the Confederates rolled up their flank. Dieckmann's two guns fired, but before they could reload, musketry downed their horses and they had to abandon the guns. The 54th NY broke before the charging Confederates, and the fledgling 153rd PA faced the Georgians alone. Then they broke. The charge washed over Von Gilsa's positions, hitting Devens' flank. In minutes Von Gilsa lost 264 men, including half his regimental commanders.

Confusion in the woods was complete. The Confederates were supposed to be to their front, and here they were being hit from the right flank in thick woods at twilight when friend and foe were both gray shapes against the dark woods.

Colonel Lee of the 55th Ohio went to headquarters at the Talley Farm and requested permission to change facing and meet the advance. General Devens, later said to be drunk, refused to give the order. Colonel Lee returned to his command, saw the situation was worse, and returned again to ask Devens if he could redeploy. Again Devens refused.

Colonel Reily of the 75th Ohio was Devens' reserve. When he saw the situation, he charged without orders. His decisive action made some of Gilsa's men rally and charge with him, but his unit was too small. O'Neal's Alabamians overlapped his right and Doles overlapped his left. Stuart's horse artillery joined the fray, blasting canister into the 75th Ohio, killing Reily. The 75th's resistance collapsed. In the next few minutes, Devens' line folded.

Iverson's North Carolinians on the left flank advanced, turning the surprised Union troops they encountered. The 20th North Carolina broke into camp, charged through campfires and over stacked weapons, and pursuing the fleeing Yankees with singular purpose. Heth commented that at Wilderness Church, "I passed... a line of muskets stacked... 200 yards in length." The 38th North Carolina surged ahead.

Confederates paused briefly to grab cooking food or snatch booty abandoned by the routing Union soldiers before continuing their pursuit. The advance moved almost as fast as men could run. In the heat of battle, success flushed the Southerners, and gradually the Confederate left flank was starting to outdistance the Confederate right flank commanded by Colquitt, who was cautiously advancing to protect his right flank.

Meanwhile Devens' men routed into Schurz's division. Schurz's men stalled the Confederate advance a few minutes. Schurz had placed three of his

Henry Heth was a friend of Lee's and is said to be the only general in the Army of Northern Virginia that Lee addressed by his first name. He commanded the Light Division when Hill was wounded.

With Rodes leading the assault, E.A. O'Neal took over command of Rodes' unit and was in the first wave of Jackson's men to fall on the unsuspecting XI Corps.

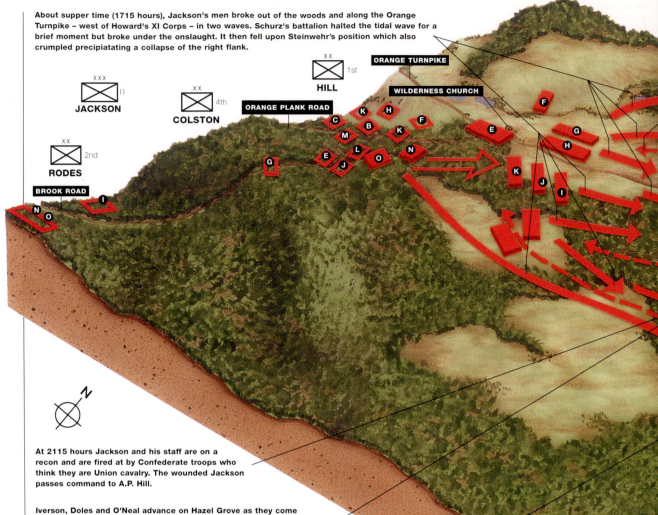

About supper time (1715 hours), Jackson's men broke out of the woods and along the Orange Turnpike – west of Howard's XI Corps – in two waves. Schurz's battalion halted the tidal wave for a brief moment but broke under the onslaught. It then fell upon Steinwehr's position which also crumpled precipiatating a collapse of the right flank.

ORANGE TURNPIKE

HILL 1st

WILDERNESS CHURCH

JACKSON XXX II

COLSTON XX 4th

ORANGE PLANK ROAD

RODES XX 2nd

BROOK ROAD

At 2115 hours Jackson and his staff are on a recon and are fired at by Confederate troops who think they are Union cavalry. The wounded Jackson passes command to A.P. Hill.

Iverson, Doles and O'Neal advance on Hazel Grove as they come under fire from Fairview Knoll. Confederate artillery later arrives and conducts counter-battery fire and Confederate troops assault the Union artillery park, finally taking the position after fierce hand-to-hand fighting.

The 8th Pennsylvania cavalry pulls out from Fairview and blunders into advancing Confederates before breaking free and returning to Union lines with severe losses.

The Union troops close ranks and form a defensive line with Sickles and Barlow pulling back from a salient which would be undefensible had they remained.

CONFEDERATES
A Lane
B Jones
C Pender
D Heth
E Ramseur
F Iverson
G Paxton
H Nicholls
I McGowan
J Colquitt
K O'Neal
L Doles
M Warren
N Thomas
O Archer
*For a full detailed unit description
see ORDER OF BATTLE page 32*

BATTLE OF CHANCELLORSVILLE

2 May 1863, 1700 - 2000, viewed from the south-east. Having finalised their plans throughout the night, Jackson's corps numbering some 28,000 men undertook their daring flanking march during the day, which placed them at the weakest point of the Union line. As dusk set in, they launched their attack against the unprepared troops of Howard's corps which quickly turned into a pell mell route of the whole Federal flank.

Southern troops fall back and reform – as their waves and units are intermixed – between 1900-2130 hours, so they can conduct an effective night assault on the Union positions.

Confederate pursuit is now fast and furious, almost a foot race as fleeing Yankees run toward Hooker's Headquarters seeking shelter from the rebel storm. Rodes was everywhere at once urging his men on, "Over friend or foe".

Iverson's North Carolinians on the left flank make good progress, driving the enemy from their camps. Taking a brief rest they charge on into the fleeing mass of blue and soon outdistance the simultaneous attack of the right flank under Colquitt.

Sensing danger on his right flank from reports of Union cavalry in the vacinity, Colquitt advances piecemeal until he is completely out of sync with the timetable Jackson had laid down for the attack. Many Union troops under Slocum manage to escape and now had time to formulate some kind of defence near to Chancellorsville on Fairview Knoll.

ELY'S FORD ROAD

BULLOCK ROAD

CHANCELLOR HOUSE

HAZEL GROVE

FAIRVIEW KNOLL

TO FREDRICKSBURG

ORANGE PLANK ROAD

Taken by surprise at his HQ, Howard attempted to rally his men around the flag but this had little effect. Retreating Union troops slammed into those behind them and the entire Union line threatened to collapse.

The easternmost units – although swamped by the fleeing troops of XI corps – form a tenuous defensive line which is holding by 2000 hours as the fog rolls in once more.

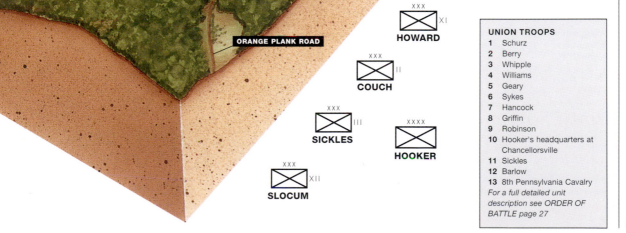

XXX XI
HOWARD

XXX II
COUCH

XXX III
SICKLES

XXXX
HOOKER

XXX XII
SLOCUM

UNION TROOPS
1 Schurz
2 Berry
3 Whipple
4 Williams
5 Geary
6 Sykes
7 Hancock
8 Griffin
9 Robinson
10 Hooker's headquarters at Chancellorsville
11 Sickles
12 Barlow
13 8th Pennsylvania Cavalry
For a full detailed unit description see ORDER OF BATTLE page 27

55

General Amiel T. Whipple was commanding one of Sickles' units when a Confederate sniper sighted him and fired, hitting him seriously. Transported to Washington, he died – the second one of Sickles' III Corps commanders killed by a Southern marksman.

Lieutenant-Colonel Frank Huger commanded Alexander's battalion after Alexander became acting chief of artillery. He served through Petersburg. His men boasted that they never ran, and that after every battle they buried their own dead.

OPPOSITE **Taken just shortly after the battle of Chancellorsville, this spot shows blasted trees and heavy woods north of the trail Jackson was following when he was shot.**

regiments facing west – the 58th NY, 82nd Ohio, and 26th Wisconsin. They stood and poured fire into the Confederate juggernaut, but even that was not enough to stop the onrushing horde of Jackson's men pursuing the fleeing Union soldiers. Schurz's division collapsed back into Steinwehr's. Artillery caissons added to the confusion, with panicked horses and riders shattering Union lines, running east, effectively turning the Union right flank and collapsing it. Most Union resistance was futile.

One Union unit which stood was Dilger's Battery I of the 1st Ohio. Dilger's six Napoleons fired steadily into Jackson's oncoming legions. When the Confederates were within a hundred yards, Dilger limbered, retreated, unlimbered and fired again. That stalled the advance. The Confederates ignored the fleeing German troops and concentrated instead on the artillery, shooting the horses and making the artillerymen abandon the guns. Private Darwin Cody of Dilger's battery summed up Union feeling on the lack of infantry support for the artillery when he said, "Damn the Dutch!"

Howard attempts to stem the flood

When Howard heard the row, he asked what was happening, and was told his men were routing. Seeing the retreating troops he said, "Such a mass of fugitives I haven't seen since Bull Run." Grabbing the colors and mounting, he clamped the flag with the stump of his right arm and galloped toward the firing and the mass of retreating men, hoping to inspire and rally them. He may have been unprepared, but he was brave.

Howard's appearance had little effect on the retreating soldiers until he encountered part of Bushbeck's brigade, the 154th NY. The 154th stood. Fragments of other units rallied with them, occupying rifle pits near Dowdall's Tavern which faced west. There were 4,000 Yankees. Volleys cut "roads" through the onrushing Confederates, who would then re-form and commence their advance again. The Union infantry held up the Confederate advance for almost half an hour, and then they too broke under the relentless momentum of Jackson's men.

If there was a problem, it was that the Southern advance was too fast. Rodes was everywhere on his horse, urging all who could hear him to advance, "Over friend or foe." Individually, soldiers stopped to fire and became separated from their units; Colston's advancing support units merged with Rodes' troops. The problem accentuated as A.P. Hill's men moved up. The Southern forces were hopelessly mixed within an hour, but all advanced steadily.

Colquitt was still nervous. He thought he sighted Union cavalry to his right and slowed his advance, facing his men south. Ramseur was behind Colquitt, and he fumed at the needless and overly cautious delay. Eventually Colquitt resumed his advance, but the damage to Jackson's carefully laid out timetable of advance had been done. The units were out of sync, allowing many Union troops to escape which otherwise would have been captured.

Seeing some units outdistancing others, Jackson rode with his men, crying, "Press, press them!" Jackson paused at one point to congratulate Beckham's horse artillery, and then he complimented Rodes on his success. Jackson thanked God for his victory. In an hour and a half his men had pressed the Union XI Corps well over a mile from its initial position. They were within two miles of Hooker's headquarters at Chancellorsville. But daylight was fast fading.

Unformed, the men of XI Corps routed, fleeing. They ran into Sickles' Corps, which folded on itself and had to fight long and hard to re-form even a semblance of a line. By the time the Union had a tenuous line, it was 2000 hours and the fog was rolling back in.

Major Huey's 8th PA cavalry was unaware of the exact situation with XI Corps. Darkness gathered. They were waiting at Hazel Grove for orders to pursue what they thought were retreating Southerners. He was ordered to find stragglers and help them rejoin their commands. Using a road moving northward and then east, he began to see shadowy figures which he assumed to be stragglers. He did

Hiram Berry was a brave Federal officer who rallied his men on the Turnpike and held up the Southern advance. He was killed while crossing the road to relay orders.

not expect to find Southern infantry, and certainly did not anticipate running into the Confederate advance. Moving east on the road, he encountered the faltering advance of Rodes' men, finally recognizing them as the enemy. Huey could not turn without exposing his men needlessly, so he decided to charge, break through, and once on the Plank Road, force his way east to Chancellorsville. Southerner fire shattered his charge. Part of the 8th veered into the woods. Three officers near Huey were killed. Huey forced his way north. The 8th PA lost 76 men.

Meanwhile Hooker told General Hiram Berry to "receive the enemy on your bayonets." A half mile west of Chancellorsville, Berry formed his line and waited, staring into the gathering darkness. Meade formed V Corps along the north edge of Mineral Springs Road toward Reynolds, who guarded U.S. Ford. General Alpheus Williams of Slocum's XII Corps extended the Union line down the Plank Road, linking up with Berry's left. This completed the isolation of the XI Corps positions. It was 2100 hours.

Berry and Hays turned their men with difficulty. They rallied some of the closer XI Corps units and met the onrushing Confederates with musket fire and bayonets. The Confederate advance slowed. Sickles turned his attention to Jackson, and with Pleasonton's cavalry at Hazel Grove Hill and Union batteries emplaced on Fairview Knoll, Jackson found his advance enfiladed by Union fire coming from his right.

Jackson had not gained as much ground as he wanted, and although he knew the Union had formed a defensive line, he was aware of how unsettled that line was. Even though it was misty and there would be fog later, the moon was high and gave off enough light for night operations. He knew of Sickles' earlier predicament and hoped to exploit it.

A terrible price for victory

Jackson ordered his commanders to take time to reform and try to realign. Rodes and Colston would regroup and A.P. Hill would assume the front, preparing for a night assault. When Hill asked Jackson what he should do, Jackson replied, "Press them; cut them off from the United States Ford, Hill."

While his commanders regrouped, Jackson would take his staff and assess the situation. A private in the 9th VA cavalry, David Kyle, had grown up in the area and knew it well. He would guide Jackson's reconnaissance.

With evening fog came the damp. Jackson pulled on his raincoat as protection. So far there was moonlight to enable Jackson to review Union positions, because he was certain the unsteady Union troops would give way if he could just find the right place to push them. It was 2100 hours.

With his staff, Jackson began scouting the back roads, looking for a weakness or an opening for Hill that would let him advance and totally rout the Army of the Potomac. As usual, Jackson gave little thought to his own safety or how exposed his staff would be in the no-man's land between Union and Confederate lines. Occasional shots, followed by nervous bursts of musketry, broke the early evening stillness. Aware of the presence of Union cavalry because of the 8th Pennsylvanian's earlier charge, Confederate pickets were alert for the sound of horses approaching from the north or east.

HOWARD ATTEMPTS TO RALLY XI CORPS When Howard heard the commotion of the routing troops from Von Gilsa's brigade, he ran outside to see what the situation was. Upon discovering that his corps' flank had been turned by the Confederates who were pouring out of the woods, he realized the scale of his misjudgement. Mounting his horse, he clamped the flag with the stump of his right arm, and rode toward the mass of fleeing Union soldiers in an attempt to stem the retreat.

ABOVE **This gives the reader a small feel for a Federal reserve battery of light artillery, such as those who held Hazel Grove or Fairview.**

BELOW, RIGHT **Little Sorrel was Jackson's favorite horse. After Jackson was wounded, the horse bolted but was recaptured. Later Little Sorrel was stabled by an admirer of Jackson's until the horse's death.**

A mile east of Dowdall's, the Mountain Road went north. Jackson's party advanced at a walk. Ahead he heard sounds of men preparing barricades: Union lines. Turning, Jackson headed the scouting party back toward Confederate positions.

Men of the 18th North Carolina heard approaching hoofbeats. They called out passwords, aware of the possibility of a Union probe or attack. There was no counter-sign. Nervously they shot into the dark, fearing a Union attack, firing several volleys before an officer ordered them to cease fire – they were shooting their own troops!

LEFT **Taken just after the battle, this picture shows all that remained of the Chancellor House after the fire which destroyed it shortly after Hooker moved his headquarters.**

The damage was done. Jackson was severely wounded in his left lower and upper arm and his right hand. He was bleeding profusely from a severed blood vessel in his upper arm, and a tourniquet was applied. Litter bearers were enlisted and carried the pain-wracked Jackson away from the scene. When inquiring who was on the litter, soldiers were told, "a Confederate officer." It would harm morale to let the men know that Jackson was down. One man recognized Jackson on the litter, and the words flitted fearfully along the lines: Stonewall was down. Hill is in command, Jackson ordered, forgetting Hill's feud with him and recognizing that the South's need for an experienced commander was more important than his pride. After passing command, Jackson allowed himself to be removed from the field.

A.P. Hill briefly commanded the corps until wounded by shrapnel, which kept him from walking. Although far from mortal, the wound was disabling, and Hill passed over Rodes, who he felt was too inexperienced to command a corps and put Stuart in command. Stuart, a cavalry officer, had never commanded infantry. Standing and fighting, slogging ahead despite shot and shell is different from hitting and running, from probing and then galloping away if the enemy appears to have the advantage. Despite that, Hill passed command to Stuart.

From the time he arrived on the field, J.E.B. Stuart was aggressive. Lee sent him a message telling him to move with decision. "The enemy... must be pressed... dispossess them of Chancellorsville. I will join you as soon as I can... but let nothing delay ... driving the enemy... from his positions."

At a house near Dowdall's Tavern, Dr. Maguire administered first aid to the wounded general. Then Jackson was moved to the field hospital located near Dowdall's Tavern. Shortly after 0200 at the field hospital Maguire amputated Jackson's left arm. After Jackson regained consciousness, he was removed to Guiney's Station at the rear of the Southern position. There he was placed in a room at the Chandler's plantation office.

The arm would start to heal but he would pass away in little more than a week from complications brought on by pneumonia.

When he first heard of Jackson's wound, Lee said, "Victory is dearly bought which deprives us of the services of General Jackson even for a short time."

A.P. Hill was a proud man who had a feud with Jackson over a slight. When Jackson was wounded, Hill briefly commanded II Corps until a debilitating wound caused him to relinquish command just when he was most needed.

JACKSON IS WOUNDED

On a reconnaissance mission after the attack of that day, Jackson and his staff found themselves between the Union and Confederate lines as they searched for a weak spot in the enemy's defences. At 2130 hours, nervous pickets from the 18th Carolina heard the approaching party and when their challenge went unanswered fired several volleys toward them. With one man dead and others injured Jackson himself was severely wounded, and it was some time before it was possible to get him back to the Confederate lines for his wounds to be assessed

DAY THREE AND BEYOND

Stuart on the offensive

At 0330 hours 3 May, Stuart received Lee's message telling him to press the enemy back and then unite with him. In the previous night's disorganized state that had been feasible; however, the Union Army had reformed overnight so that Stuart no longer overlapped their lines and they now stood as a barrier between him and Lee.

The Union position included a large, three-sided salient. Almost a square formed of Couch and Slocum's corps while Reynolds and Meade's commands projected north of the salient to the ford, and Sickles' command formed a northwest-facing line at Hazel Grove. These positions made I Corps and V Corps reserves. Howard's shattered command was slowly reforming north of Couch and south of Meade, away from the Southerners. Hooker held Chancellorsville, but with the separate Confederate commands pushing north and east, it was doubtful he could retain this position without a general Union counter-offensive.

At least Hooker's artillery was safe for the time being. Hazel Grove and Fairview were the same height, rising above the blanket of trees and in view of each other, allowing reciprocal artillery support.

Chancellorsville and Fairview lay within Federal lines. Federal artillery was covering the front from Fairview Knoll. Hazel Grove was outside Union lines and therefore an attractive target. More importantly, as a natural artillery park, it was a strategic position to occupy, but neither side yet realized how important it was. Sickles sent to Hooker asking to extend the lines to include Hazel Grove, but

A shell crater on Marye's Heights showing damage similar to the one which hit the column at the Chancellor house and stunned Hooker landed here. This one killed several horses and destroyed these waiting caissons.

General William T. Wofford came to Wilcox's aid on the Orange Turnpike. Together with Kershaw, they stood at Salem Church, south of the Turnpike, and stopped Sedgwick's advance.

Joseph B. Kershaw was a South Carolinian who served in every action with the Army of Northern Virginia from First Manassas to Appomattox. True to form, he led his men in the thick of the fighting at Salem Church.

Hooker was asleep and his chief of staff refused to wake him. Sickles fretted while Hooker snoozed.

Lee's line began a mile and a quarter east of Chancellorsville, its right end covering the Orange Turnpike; stretching southwest it crossed the Plank Road with Wofford, Semmes, and Kershaw holding that ground, extending east and south of Hooker. To the west of the Plank Road Anderson faced north with Wright and Posey protecting the left flank, facing northwest and due west respectively.

To the west, the Orange Turnpike bisected Stuart's command. Now as consolidated as he could make it, his corps had advanced east almost to Bullock Road. Heth led, commanding Hill's division. Behind him Colston's men followed. Farthest west was Rodes' division.

Jackson had blessed Stuart's appointment and had mumbled that Stuart should do "what he thinks best." Stuart, although seemingly an unsuitable commander, may have been the best choice to assume Jackson's command. Like Lee and Jackson, he understood the primary directive of striking before the enemy could strike. His problem was the mixed status of his units. It was hopeless to attempt to sort them out in the dark.

At dawn Stuart ordered Lane, Archer, and McGowan to take their brigades forward, straightening their lines as they advanced and moving at right angles to the Turnpike. By 0530 they were on the move. Archer's men encountered stout resistance. Archer did not straighten his line, and consequently McGowan was not in position either. Archer lost contact with McGowan and forged ahead, moving uphill and entering a deforested glade 1,200 yards ahead, which was the entrance to Hazel Grove.

The fight for Fairview

Sickles had held the grove all night, but at dawn Hooker visited and saw it as a salient – the very sort of salient Sickles would gravitate toward at Gettysburg with devastating results. Hooker was interested in defense, and ordered Sickles to abandon Hazel Grove. Sickles reluctantly obeyed, and Archer's Confederates gratefully moved into the soon-to-be-Southern artillery park.

Archer's troops met light resistance from Sickles' rearguard. Graham's Pennsylvanians, who were supporting Huntington's battery on Hazel Grove, were in turn supported by Union troops firing from Fairview Knoll. The unimpeded Union artillery shredded Archer's men, stalling their advance. Confederate riflemen volleyed and eventually drove off the Pennsylvanians, and Archer re-formed. His unit then charged and took the position, along with 100 Union prisoners. It was 0630 hours.

Confederate artillery commander E. Porter Alexander scouted the position and recognized Hazel Grove as the ideal artillery park from which to slam round after round into Hooker's line and against the Union artillery on Fairview. Lee ordered 30 guns to occupy the position and support the attack.

Fairview and the area below it were well fortified. Multiple lines of breastworks provided fall-back positions: in the event that one was overrun, another lay behind. Coupled with the heavy brush and rolling terrain, Union soldiers improved upon the natural fortress with deadfalls, rifle pits and abatis to slow the oncoming Southerners. Virtually four lines of Union troops manned the defenses. However, because of the brush, support of units other than to the immediate right or left was difficult. Because of the slope of the knoll, the Federal guns could do little to support Union troops closely packed below, and they had to content themselves with firing over the heads of the combatants and into the distant woods where they could see Confederates moving.

Meanwhile McGowan's men ran into the position occupied by the 37th NY. After volleyed rifle duels, the 1st South Carolina bogged down when they encountered Williams' supporting Federals. Ruger's 3rd brigade charged and flanked McGowan, which drove them back to the first Union line. Lane's 7th, 18th, 28th, and 33rd North Carolinians charged the 3rd Maryland, sending its raw recruits fleeing before the wildly yelling Southerners. Lane's troops overran Dimick's guns, but were brought up short by murderous massed artillery fire.

Major William Pegram rushed batteries of Confederate artillery to Hazel Grove so he could start laying fire into the Union lines. Pender's brigade hit Hiram Berry's Federals on the Orange Turnpike, driving the 1st Massachusetts and 74th NY back. Berry stopped the rout, and put his troops into some semblance of order, positioning them across the road where they could pour fire into the advancing Confederates. Crossing the hailstorm of gunfire which swept the road, Berry made it to the other side where he conferred with Gershom Mott to decide on a defensive plan. On the return trip, a sharpshooter saw the general and fired. Berry fell, and died less than five minutes later.

North of the road, the 13th North Carolina and Thomas's Georgians met little artillery fire and charged, forcing the Union units back. Their charge was so successful that 1st Lt. John R. Ireland captured Brig. Hays and his staff before they could escape. The Confederate surge threatened Union artillery on Fairview Knoll but Franklin's brigade placed themselves between the Southerners and the Union artillery. At the same time Brig.Gen. French turned his men so they were oblique to the road and charged Thomas's rear and flank, sending Thomas reeling in retreat to the first Union line. Cosgrove's Indianans forced the Confederates over the abatis and then poured deadly rifle fire into the huddled masses who tried to get back over the first line to continue the hand-to-hand fight. After a couple of minutes, only the 28th North Carolina still withstood the withering Union small arms fire. The rest had broken and retreated to the safety of the woods where they could re-form.

Stuart was on the scene, seeming to be everywhere at once, urging weary and faltering soldiers forward into the maelstrom of fire again and again. He

HAZEL GROVE, 3 MAY 1863

ABOVE **General James Lane was in Hill's division. His men were in the third line of attack on XI Corps, arrayed north of the Turnpike in column. On the Plank Road 198 men of the 128th PA surrendered to his unit.**

The fight for Hazel Grove. Jackson's flank attack forced Hooker to consolidate his forces, forming a line remarkably like a cow's udder, with its lowest point at Hazel Grove, which Sickles held. By withdrawing again in the face of Lee's attack, Hooker vacated the best artillery ground in the area for Alexander to organize counter-battery fire against Fairview, thus forcing the Union to abandon Chancellorsville cross-roads and ultimately Fairview itself.

commended the 28th for their courage and urged them forward. Like the gallant 600, the 28th advanced, only to fall back bloodied and battered. A third time he rallied and sent them forward. They came reeling back, proud but bloodied. Abner Perrin moved his unit forward with 10,000 other Confederates. They took the first Union line and had partly captured another before the massed artillery and musketry stalled their attack. Stuart swallowed the bitter pill that a single Confederate division could not carry the day.

Major William Pegram added 20 guns along the Plank Road to the weight of metal thrown against the Union on Fairview knoll. Realizing that the Confederacy had numerical artillery superiority, Pegram shouted to E. Porter Alexander, "Colonel, a glorious day!" The Union guns replied, but ammunition was running low, and the rate of fire slowed. Best's Union artillery continued to blast round after round into the Confederates until his infantry support withdrew, and then he began to consider withdrawal.

Stuart ordered his second and third lines – Rodes and Colston's units – forward. More than two dozen Confederate artillery pieces supported their attack, plowing deep furrows into the tightly packed men on Hooker's flank. Paxton's Stonewall brigade went through a meat grinder as it moved forward, trying to set an example and rally the 13th South Carolina. The 2nd VA on the right with the 4th VA, and with the 27th VA following them, came under heavy fire. The 2nd and 4th moved apart and in the gap between them the men of the 27th were hit by Union fire. Knowing he had to prevent the attack from stalling, Paxton ran between his units to keep the attack moving ahead, but fell with a mortal chest wound. Stuart's second line was shot to pieces and demoralized by the severe resistance.

Stuart had one last hole-card: Rodes. Stuart ordered Rodes forward, and Lt.Col. Hilary Jones massed artillery fire at the Federal counter-attack which had driven Thomas and Pender backward. Stuart's third line passed by the remnants of the first two lines. Colonel O'Neal was wounded as his unit passed through the hailstorm of Federal artillery. Bonham, of the 3rd Alabama, led the charge up Fairview knoll with little resistance, but when they crossed the abatis, Union small arms fire blasted their charge into disarray and drove them back.

Doles' Georgians and Ramseur's North Carolinians advanced. Ramseur saw the stalled troops who had gone before him, and tried to enlist the aid of these demoralized members of the first and second waves that were huddled beneath the shellfire overhead. No one listened to his pleading. He asked permission from Stuart to advance over the huddled men. Stuart told him to give the order, and the North Carolinians advanced purposefully, ignoring the bullets whizzing by them to impact Graham's flank. His assault ran into a wall of shot and his advance faltered.

Finally Stuart taunted and exhorted the weary men to remember Jackson, and got the attack started again. The Stonewall Brigade crossed the earthworks,

Brigadier General E. Porter Alexander was one of only three Southern generals of artillery. When Jackson began his flank march, Alexander realized from reports of artillery fire that Union forces were massing near Chancellorsville.

BELOW **On 2 May, just after dawn, Knap's Pennsylvania battery, which was stationed near Chancellorsville and armed with 10 lb Parrott rifles, engaged in counter-battery fire with ten guns from Pegram's battery, destroying two Confederate caissons.**

ignoring the air filled with bullets and artillery rounds. The 12th Georgia moved forward; the 30th North Carolina, which had been protecting the guns, joined the advance, hitting the Union flank. The Union troops retreated, moving three-quarters of a mile, nearly to Chancellorsville. There, Paxton and Ramseur's men paused, almost out of ammunition, while other Confederates surged past them. Of 340 men who had begun the assault, the 2nd North Carolina had lost 214; Ramseur had started with nearly 1,400 men and lost 633.

Doles fared better. About 0915 hours part of his men gained the second line of Union earthworks and then turned north. Finding himself to the rear of two Union units, he then charged Best's unsuspecting men.

Meanwhile, at 0915 hours Hooker was leaning against a column of the Chancellor house when an artillery round hit it. Flung to the ground by the impact, Hooker was insensible, and appeared badly injured at first. Slowly the stunned commander arose, groggy and disoriented. His first thought was to reassure his troops, and still reeling from the close call, he mounted and rode his white horse where his troops could see him. Then he followed his staff's advice and moved his headquarters to the Bullock place, where he convalesced and took a dram of the good stuff. Hooker summoned Darius Couch, and although Couch hoped Hooker would relinquish command, Hooker merely wanted him there as a conduit for his orders. Couch later noted that Hooker seemed detached but lucid.

At 0930 hours on Fairview, Best's remaining units were surprised when Doles' gray-clad infantry surged up seemingly from under their feet. Best later said, "Our right and left turned,... the enemy musketry... so advanced as to pick off our men and horses, I was compelled to withdraw my guns to save them." The surprise appearance of Doles' men resulted in the capture of many prisoners. Then, protected by the slope of Fairview Knoll, Doles flanked the Union artillery and captured seven field pieces which were not fast enough withdrawing. The Union rallied and counter-attacked, but Doles drove them off, holding his position until Union artillery at Chancellorsville forced him off the knoll.

Anderson and McLaws pressed Geary and Hancock's positions from the south. Geary and Hancock's men yielded ground grudgingly. The Confederate onslaught, coupled with Stuart's offensive, put many Union units back to back

with other Union units. If the Union troops broke or gave way, they could only flee north. Chancellorsville was rapidly becoming untenable.

Hooker abandons Chancellorsville

Assessing the situation, Hooker realized with a sinking heart the full extent of the Confederate deception and success – and the failure of his master plan. He ordered Couch to withdraw the army from Chancellorsville between 0945 and 1000 hours. At 1000 hours, Union troops received orders to abandon Fairview Knoll. Suddenly Hancock, Couch and Slocum found themselves fighting a rearguard action. Hooker had still not committed the sorely needed I, V, or XI Corps reserves, and bitterly the rearguard commanders realized that this was the commander Lincoln had reminded to use "all his troops."

When Lee and Stuart realized Hooker was withdrawing, they were thrilled: not only could they unite, but their enemy was again yielding ground to them. With the enemy fleeing in disarray, could they capitalize on their good fortune and pursue in strength to inflict severe damage on the disorganized superior force?

Confederate artillery fire had damaged Chancellorsville. Despite the damp, the woods were filled with dry leaves, fast-burning softwood trees, and masses of deadfalls which ignited. As Hooker withdrew, the woods west of Chancellorsville and soon the building itself were ablaze. Lee, mounted on Traveller, led his armies forward while the flames surged through the piney thickets, and the screams of the wounded turned to shrieks as the greedy flames reached them. There was little either army could do to help those trapped by the flames. As Chancellorsville was engulfed, it no doubt seemed an allegory for all of Northern Virginia these last three years. Lee stopped Traveller for a moment just inside the clearing, and surveyed the scene before him, slumping slightly in his saddle as he witnessed the terrible price of victory. Jackson had made this possible, he realized, both the pain and the elation. Then he squared his shoulders and stared at the northern treeline: he must pursue the Army of the Potomac and, if at all possible, complete its destruction. His problem was that his forces were committed and tired. Where would he find fresh troops to drive the Yankees clear back to Washington?

Paxton was a rising star, promoted over the heads of many Confederates to command of Jackson's Stonewall Brigade. On 3 May his premonition of death was realized while attacking the redoubts when a Minie ball killed him instantly.

HOOKER IS INJURED

Whilst at his headquarters near Chancellorsville, Hooker was assessing the events of the previous day, and Stuart's offensive of that morning on his defensive positions. A Confederate shell landed nearby him as he stood on the porch, knocking him stunned to the ground. Although slightly concussed, he was unhurt and continued to issue orders to his troops, even though some of his command believed he should step down.

Sedgwick's triumph at Fredericksburg

Back at Fredericksburg the long static situation was about to change as the dormant Sedgwick at last roused himself and plodded forward. Had he acted more quickly, perhaps the Union could still have smashed Lee's army.

On 1 May Lee had left Early at Fredericksburg and when he realized that Hooker was trying some sleight of hand to steal a march and surprise him, Lee had told Early to do whatever he could to hold Sedgwick in place. Early had paid attention to Lee's admonition to retreat toward Richmond if Sedgwick advanced and he was faced with "overpowering numbers." On the other hand, if Sedgwick retired to east of the river, Early was to move west and support Lee.

Sedgwick seemed content to stay where he was and as long as Early remained, Sedgwick seemed to believe the ruse and feel that Lee's entire army was held in place. On 2 May Col. Chilton of Lee's staff brought Early orders. Chilton misrepresented them and Early thought he was being ordered to move west and support Lee at once, regardless of the situation developing at Fredericksburg. Still, Sedgwick's forces seemed quiet, and Chilton's interpretation of Lee's directive was not totally outside the scope of Early's previous orders. Leaving Barksdale in command of a small force at Fredericksburg, Early struck off on the Orange Plank Road to help Lee. Barksdale felt he had too few men to stop a concentrated Union offensive.

Hooker sent Sedgwick orders to advance past Fredericksburg with all due speed and attack Lee's rear. Brigadier Govenour K. Warren relayed his command and made certain Sedgwick appreciated how strongly Hooker wanted him to advance. His defensive plan was to catch Lee between Couch and Sedgwick and crush him; then they would defeat Jackson. By the time Sedgwick moved, however, Lee and Stuart had linked up the Confederate command.

Sedgwick commanded nearly 24,000 men, Gibbon another 3,500, and at best, Early had nearly 9,000 men. At worst, Sedgwick outnumbered Early by three to one; and although slow, at least Sedgwick was in action. Warren later confided to Hooker that he doubted whether Sedgwick would have acted if he had not been present to goad him forward. To make matters more difficult, Col. Sharpe of

Military Intelligence notified Sedgwick not to use telegraph or visuals as the Confederates could presumably read them.

On 3 May at 0700 hours Gibbon anchored Sedgwick's right on the Rappahannock. Brooks, Newton, and Howe's units were strung from Fredericksburg across to Deep Run. Early's troops overlapped VI Corps. Barksdale held the Southern left flank, and the majority of Early's men were on the heights above the spot of Burnside's abortive December assault. The Washington (La.) Artillery supported Barksdale. Harry Hays' Louisianans shifted to just north of Barksdale, with their right flank on the Orange Plank Road and north of Marye's Heights. Wilcox held the far northern River Road a quarter of a mile west of the canal and was heading toward Hays' position. At 0700 hours the Union assault against Barksdale's position began.

Barksdale sent Early word of the Federal advance. He hoped to hold until Early arrived. When Early heard of Sedgwick's attack, he decided to countermarch to his former position. Barksdale's men waited behind the stone wall, fingers tight around their rifles.

Union units, among them the 5th WI, 6th ME, and 7th MA, raged against the stone wall, attacking in two waves. The Confederates decimated them, wiping out between 33% and 40% of the attacking units. The Union advance stalled as the ground before the wall became layered with casualties and wounded. During a lull, Col. Griffin of the 18th MS allowed Federals to approach outside the wall at his lines under a flag of truce to aid fallen Union soldiers. The Federal soldiers helping the wounded discovered that relatively few Confederates held more than three times their number of opponents at bay, and the Federals passed this information back to their superiors.

Because of this new information, a third attack on the heights took place. Colonel Thomas Allen of the 5th WI told his men, "When the signal... is

Sedgwick and his staff. When he broke through Barksdale's line, he thought he was going to link up with Hooker. Unknown to him, Hooker was planning his withdrawal and evidently had no intention of supporting Sedgwick's advance.

PHASE 1 After repeated attempts, Barksdale's men who are spread thin but are positioned behind a stone wall which ran along the edge of the ridge repulses Newton's initial attack at 1000 hours. The Union requests a truce and are allowed to send men to give aid to their wounded who lie scattered about the wall and base of the heights. Union soldiers see how thinly defended the walls are and report back to their commanders.

PHASE 2 Wilcox sees the line crumbling and tries to enlist aid but is unsuccessful and retires west down the Orange Turnpike. Other Confederate units start down Telegraph Road to follow Early but turn back to return to Fredericksburg when Sedgwick abandons the heights later in the day.

PHASE 3 1030 hours, Sedgewick now starts to move down the Orange Road to relieve Hooker at Chancellorsville as ordered. Unfortunately, he hesitates to allow fresh troops to lead the advance which costs the Union advance precious time.

TO FALMOUTH

ORANGE TURNPIKE

RAILWAY
RICHMOND–POTOMAC

TELEGRAPH ROAD

X
I ⊠ 5th
WILCOX

XX
⊠ II
BARKSDALE

N

SEDGWICK'S ASSAULT ON BARKSDALE'S POSITION AT MARYE'S HEIGHTS

3 May 1863, 0900 - 1100, viewed from the south-west. Receiving confusing orders from Lee's staff officer, Early had moved his forces to aid Lee in the west leaving Barksdale in command of the heights. Sedgewick had three times as many men at his disposal and under orders from Hooker to attack Lee's rear he knew he must take the heights and press on as quickly as possible.

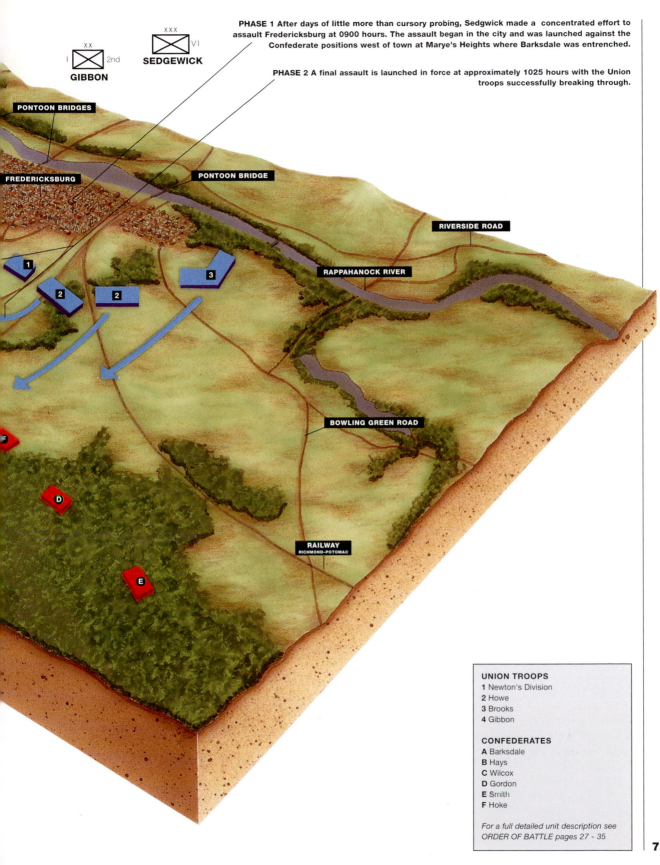

GIBBON

I XX 2nd

SEDGEWICK

XXX VI

PHASE 1 After days of little more than cursory probing, Sedgwick made a concentrated effort to assault Fredericksburg at 0900 hours. The assault began in the city and was launched against the Confederate positions west of town at Marye's Heights where Barksdale was entrenched.

PHASE 2 A final assault is launched in force at approximately 1025 hours with the Union troops successfully breaking through.

PONTOON BRIDGES

FREDERICKSBURG

PONTOON BRIDGE

RIVERSIDE ROAD

1

3

2

2

RAPPAHANOCK RIVER

BOWLING GREEN ROAD

F

D

RAILWAY
RICHMOND–POTOMAC

E

UNION TROOPS
1 Newton's Division
2 Howe
3 Brooks
4 Gibbon

CONFEDERATES
A Barksdale
B Hays
C Wilcox
D Gordon
E Smith
F Hoke

*For a full detailed unit description see
ORDER OF BATTLE pages 27 - 35*

given,... start at the double quick,... and you will not stop until you hear the order to halt. You will *never* get that order!"

Yelling and screaming defiantly, the Midwesterners charged uphill toward the stone wall. Their charge broke through the thin Southern line, capturing eight field pieces and many troops. The Washington Artillery chose to fire final rounds instead of fleeing. The Union troops overwhelmed their position. The final assault took a little over a quarter of an hour. The road to Chancellorsville lay open.

The fight at Salem Church

Jubal Early was a seasoned campaigner, and when he heard of the Union break-through, he ordered his men to start back along the Telegraph Road, which runs parallel to the Fredericksburg and Potomac railroad. Early moved toward the Cox House (on a rise) nearly two-and-a-half miles south of his former position, where an intersecting road ran west to join the Orange Plank Road. If things got dicey and he could not withstand the Union advance, he could move west. As things were, Early protected Lee's rear while moving toward the Confederate army and away from Sedgwick.

Wilcox's Alabamians arrived at Fredericksburg too late to stop the broaching of Barksdale's line. A series of ridges and gullies lies at right angles to the Orange road, providing a corduroy pattern of natural redoubts relieved only by the east-west road. If Sedgwick stopped to fight, Wilcox could buy time; if Sedgwick ignored his casualties and moved past them, he would close with Lee to relieve Hooker. Wilcox retreated along this road, using natural defenses to harass Brooks. Confederates fired, dropped back to the next ridge, formed quickly and fired again into the Federals pouring through the hole in Barksdale's lines. Sedgwick's men chose not to brush by the Alabamians, but instead stopped and fired back, thus delaying Sedgwick's advance. Falling into this take-the-next-ridge mentality, Sedgwick's advance slowed and his casualties mounted.

Despite his slowness to respond to Hooker's directives, Sedgwick was a seasoned soldier and looked to the welfare of his troops. Capturing Fredericksburg had cost him 1,000 men, mostly Newton's troops. He halted, ordered Newton's battered division to rest, and called Brooks up from the fords his men had been guarding three miles south of town. Newton's men would rest and Brooks' fresh troops would take the lead. They did not

This battlefield photo shows pontoniers erecting pontoons for Sedgwick's successful assault on 3 May. Once the bridges were up, he could send unlimited men toward the Southern positions.

Harry Hays refused to stay and fight a rearguard action against Sedgwick because his orders commanded him to retreat down Telegraph Road, and thus Wilcox was left alone to face Sedgwick.

advance until after 1500 hours with Brooks leading and Newton and Howe following.

Wilcox knew reinforcements from Chancellorsville would reach him if he could delay the Union advance. Wilcox's men fought a textbook delaying action for the next couple of hours, first holding the Federals on a ridge nearly 800 yards west of Marye's Heights and then before dropping back to a position north of the Dowman House, then west to the toll gate, and finally 1,000 yards west of that on a ridge near Salem Church. At each point they held long enough to inflict casualties, but not long enough for Sedgwick to close with all his force.

Wilcox withdrew to Salem Church and erected breastworks across the road. To the south of the road sat the red brick church, on a ridge choked with heavy undergrowth and darkened by thick woods. Only in the small clearing occupied by the church and graveyard was there room to move freely. As Wilcox prepared to meet the Union advance, Confederate reinforcements arrived, comprised of three of McLaws' brigades and one of Anderson's. Wilcox's defenses crossed the Plank Road, facing east, Semmes and Mahone were on Wilcox's right, and Kershaw and Wofford were on his left. For the South it was no longer a shoot and run situation; now was the time to stand and fight.

Around 1730 hours on 3 May, realizing that daylight was fast fading, Sedgwick could not wait for Howe to arrive. He decided to use Newton and Brooks' men to take the church and free the road. Putting Brooks astraddle the Orange Turnpike and using Newton on his right, Sedgwick attacked Salem Church.

South of the road at Salem Church that afternoon Brig.Gen. Barlett's mixed Pennsylvania, Maine, and New York regiments charged the Confederate lines. The Union troops slowly gained ground and moved closer to the church. Southern resistance was determined. Finally Col. Upton's 121st NY gained the church grounds and graveyard. The fighting was so fierce that to this day pock-marked bullet holes pit the red bricks of the church. However, Southern reinforcements under Kershaw and Wofford arrived, and their presence rallied

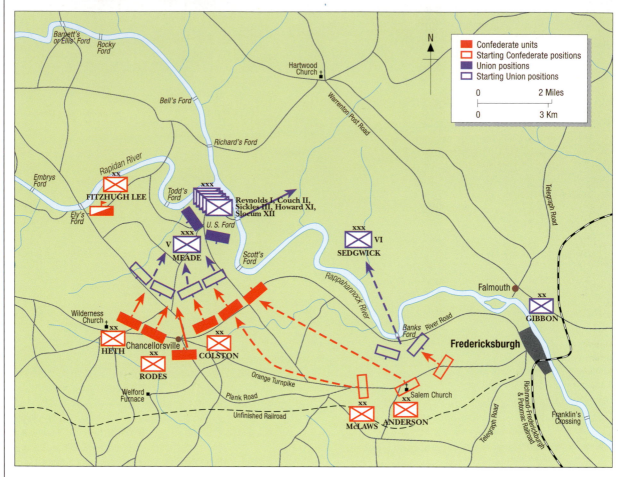

Wilcox's men, who then poured withering fire into the tired New Yorkers. Massed volleys forced the Union soldiers off church grounds and back toward the toll gate, leaving nearly a third of their force behind.

North of the road nearly 2,200 men of Brown's New Jersey brigade of Brooks' division spearheaded a thrust which Semmes and Mahone's men blunted. The Federals ran into concentrated fire and could not break through the Confederate line; their attack stalled. Firing continued until nightfall when the Union attack petered out.

That evening Howe arrived, and Sedgwick positioned Howe's men north of the Turnpike to guard his rear and flanks, facing them south and east. Hooker had promised to aid Sedgwick when he heard the sound of guns, and he wondered when Hooker would come. Wisely he guarded Banks Ford, so if he was not relieved, and if his men were sorely pressed, they could withdraw to safety. Hooker later criticized Sedgwick for failing to obey the "spirit" of his orders and attack Lee's rear. Yet throughout the day, despite the sound of Sedgwick's guns, Hooker had maintained his defensive posture and put no pressure upon Lee or Stuart to help Sedgwick. When one considers that Sedgwick's 22,000 men were being asked to rescue more than twice their own number from Lee, one realizes that although Sedgwick did not give a sterling performance, Hooker was really the one who should have been able to help him instead of insisting on fighting a defensive action.

The Southern attack shook Hooker, and he started pulling his troops even further back toward U.S. Ford. His men kept to their horseshoe-shaped defense, which delayed Confederate advances while Hooker studied the best way to

Realizing that Jackson's corps (now commanded by Stuart) was pressing him and that Lee was trying to hem him in, Hooker sent orders for Sedgwick to come to his aid. He ordered commanders to withdraw toward U.S. Ford even as he urged Sedgwick to come and help him. Fortunately Sedgwick moved slowly, or he might have found himself sacrificed as a diversion – while Hooker retreated north and east of the Rappahannock – and after taking Fredericksburg moved north for Banks Ford.

Despite being abandoned by
infantry, the Washington
Louisiana artillery fought on.
They stayed with their guns and
fell around them. Overrun, the
survivors were captured while
placing a rammer in a gun barrel
for a last shot.

Newton's men managed to
overrun Marye's Heights the third
time they tried. Newton
commented that if the
Southerners had had 1,000 more
men on the hill, he could never
have taken it.

withdraw his entire army to the safe side of the river. His priorities turned first
from attack to defense and then to preservation.

Lee heard that at Fredericksburg Sedgwick had battered Early's reinforced
division and had forced his way through the heights and was on his way toward
Chancellorsville. When he learned this, he left Stuart in command of a tiny force
to hold Hooker and marched toward Fredericksburg, after urging Early and
McLaws to cooperate against Sedgwick. McLaws was holding, but as Sedgwick's
intentions seemed to be to break through, Lee decided he needed as many men
as he could muster to face this new threat. Lee's orders to close reached Early
after dark, when it was too late to form his men for use that day. However, with
the dawn of 4 May, Early planned to attack Sedgwick.

The lost opportunity

The Confederate battle plan was simple: Early would strike at Marye's
Heights by moving north, which would either force the Union troops out of
Fredericksburg and back across the river, or cut them off and isolate the
town. McLaws would move east. Early would then swing west to link up with
McLaws to defeat Sedgwick.

Before noon on 4 May Early easily occupied Marye's Heights. There was
little Union resistance; Gibbon withdrew to the east bank toward Falmouth
to protect the Union supply depot there and at Aquia from a possible
Southern strike. Upon hearing of Early's success, Lee ordered him to move
toward Chancellorsville and hit Sedgwick's left and rear, thus closing on
McLaws and linking the army – or at the very least forcing Sedgwick to fight
two attackers.

Lee arrived at Salem Church with the remainder of Anderson's men at
about 1200 hours, confident that he could maul Sedgwick. While Anderson's
men manoeuvered, McLaws held fast and did not advance east. Early could
stretch only so far west, and thus the Confederate army could not reunite.
Most of the day was lost in inactivity or fruitless repositioning. McLaws
seemed unable or unwilling to leave his positions around Salem Church. He
had requested reinforcements from Lee, but when Lee arrived, McLaws
remained immobile while Anderson's troops, tired from marching, moved
around McLaws' right to try and link up with Early.

Aftermath

Meanwhile Sedgwick had seen gathering Confederates throughout the day. That morning, after requesting aid from Hooker, he had received orders to fall back to Fredericksburg if he could not advance and if his command was direly threatened. Sedgwick felt betrayed. He could not return to Fredericksburg because Early was on the Turnpike, cutting him off from town, so he pulled his forces slightly east and north in a horseshoe, taking care to protect his line of retreat via Banks Ford. His repositioning and the uneven terrain confused the Southerners, who moved through the dense brush slowly and expected at any minute to run into a Union division. The Confederates wasted most of the afternoon probing for Union positions. When in place and certain of Sedgwick's position, the Confederates attacked at 1800 hours, nearly 24 hours after they had forced the New Yorkers away from Salem Church.

BELOW **Marye's Heights, above Fredericksburg, was ravaged by artillery fire. Few houses remained standing, and even though civilian homes were not targets per se, many were hit by rounds in barrages.**

Wilderness Church was one of the westernmost structures along the Orange Turnpike. Close by here Jackson's rush slammed into Bushbeck and Devens' men, shattering XI Corps' defenses. After the battle Paxton was temporarily buried near here.

Earlier, under the ruse of picking up wounded men under a flag of truce, Union observers crept close enough to the wall to determine that it was not held by a massive force. Seeing a weak point they again attacked and though suffering terrible casualties from artillery and rifle fire, carried the attack up and over the wall with a bayonet charge.

The day of 4 May proved frustrating for the South. McLaws was on the Southern left flank facing a salient of Newton and Brooks' men who were the right shank and curve of Sedgwick's defense. Brooks held the center, faced by Anderson, and Early faced Howe on the Union left. Sedgwick appealed to Hooker for relief and was told, "You must not count on much assistance without I hear heavy firing." Although Sedgwick did not know it, even then Hooker was withdrawing. Had Sedgwick stood, he would have been alone. Later Couch noted that Hooker "with 80,000 men... directed Sedgwick with 22,000, to march to *his* relief... and then the whole wing [Hooker's] was withdrawn.. leaving Sedgwick to take care of himself." Sedgwick must have felt a growing sense of abandonment, although he did not know of Hooker's intentions at the time, and slowly he decided that with nightfall he would save what he could of his men.

Throughout the evening Early and Anderson slowly pushed back Sedgwick's front and left flank. Only McLaws did not move or gain ground. Hoke and Hays' men fought their way forward to Sedgwick's center, occupying a position across the Plank Road. Anderson's men made some half-hearted attacks on the right of the Union position, while McLaws sat stolidly by.

Night fell. Newton faced McLaws, but in order not to expose himself to Southern attack, he withdrew toward the crossing with the remainder of Sedgwick's corps. With night came fog. McLaws now used this as an excuse not to advance, and with the dying daylight, the Confederate hopes died.

The combination of stubborn subordinates who failed to coordinate attacks and lack of reinforcements frittered away the gains Lee had made. Under cover of night Sedgwick withdrew across the Rappahannock. He had suffered 4,500 casualties.

From his position north of the battle, Hooker could hear the fighting, but he made no effort to march to the sound of the guns. Instead he gathered his commanders and asked their opinions of the Union situation. Reynolds, Meade, and Howard wanted to attack; Couch and Sickles wanted to withdraw. After hearing his officers, Hooker let them know he intended to retreat. As he lamely explained, his primary concern was to protect Washington. Reynolds exclaimed after the meeting, "What was the use of calling us together... when he intended to retreat anyhow?" The rest of the evening, Hooker concentrated on working out how to withdraw safely to the east side of the river.

Left to right: Colonel Walter Taylor of Lee's staff; General R.E. Lee; and General G.W.C. Lee (his eldest son). This photograph was taken just after the war. Lee looks tired. Chancellorsville was his last collaboration and victory with Jackson.

As if crying for Union stupidity, rain began falling late in the night and continued through the morning of 5 May, while weary Federals crossed bridges to the east bank of the Rapidan-Rappahannock River. Some Confederate officers felt Hooker was trying to trick them with his quick and easy withdrawal in the face of a greatly outnumbered force. By 0900 on 6 May the last Union troops reached the east bank and Federal pontoniers pulled up the pontoon bridges, ending Hooker's thrust south.

The closing moves

Thereafter Hooker waited on his side of the river, anxious to capture Richmond but not anxious to cross swords with the Army of Northern Virginia again. Lee had defeated an army more than twice as large as his, but it had been costly, for with Stonewall Jackson's death, Lee had lost his "strong right arm."

Lincoln was staggered at the news of Hooker's defeat. "What will the country say?" he exclaimed. "Think of it, 130,000 magnificent soldiers cut to pieces by 60,000 half-starved ragamuffins!"

Hooker had begun this campaign confidently, but when Lee had not reacted in the manner he had supposed Lee would, self-doubt set in. Hooker became tenuous, and changed his aggressive and brash attack mode into one of defense in a strange country. When Jackson's men shattered XI Corps' position, his faltering confidence collapsed and from that point onward, Hooker's main concern was not bringing Lee to battle, but preserving his command. His value to Lincoln as a commander ended. Lincoln has said he wanted a commander who would fight, and Hooker had shown himself lacking in that respect. He had ignored the advice of his commanders to push the fight and had withdrawn. His days were numbered, for even if he had not balked when Lee later moved north in the opening moves of Gettysburg, his subordinates had lost confidence in his ability to defeat Lee, or even command an effective offensive.

Lincoln knew his army was honed, a better fighting machine than it had been, one which outnumbered and out-gunned the weary and under-supplied Confederates. He also knew that no matter how superior a sword may be, in the end it is not the sword itself but the man who wields it that determines who will be victorious. Doubtless he felt Hooker's reticence was a shadow of McClellan's earlier inability to bring the Army of the Potomac into massed battle against the Army of Northern Virginia. The army was good, but its commander had been ineffective. He must have been frustrated and angry, knowing that somewhere in the Union ranks stood an officer of Lee's equal. The question was, could he find him?

Doubtless Lee watched the Federal forces withdraw. And as he did, he savored his victory, even though it was incomplete. While looking east and north, his mind may have wandered to Antietam. The time was right for a Southern offensive. He would take the war north, and perhaps frightened Yankees would plead with Lincoln to reach a settlement. No doubt Lee felt that his star was at its zenith. If he was going north, he had to do it in the summer of 1863. He would go north and threaten Washington and Baltimore, perhaps even Harrisburg, Pennsylvania, but, sadly, he would have to do it without Jackson, his right arm. However, he would plan to move north when Longstreet arrived. As the campaign for Chancellorsville ended, the one for Gettysburg began.

Telegraph Road ran parallel to the Richmond and Fredericksburg and Potomac railroad. The road followed the riverbank for several miles south of Fredericksburg and was rutted about two feet below ground surface.

Brown's New Jersey brigade north of the church grounds spearhead a thrust which is blunted by Semmes and Mahone's men. Once againg the Federals cannot break through the rebel line, and they fall back with firing continuing until nightfall.

1540 - 1615 hours. The Alabamians withdraw to the woods, slowly giving ground to Brown's men. The Union advances slowly beyond the toll gate in the face of stiff southern small arms fire. As the Union forces approach the church, Wilcox's men charge, but are driven back by Union superior artillery and small arms fire.

WILCOX   5th

MAHONE   1st

SEMMES   1st

TO CHANCELLORSVILLE

L

K

J

I

H

G

F

E

D

C

B

A

SALEM CHURCH

14

16

15

14

South of Salem Church, Union troops of Brig.Gen.'s Bartlett's brigade had gained the church grounds and grave yard after fierce fighting. The Confederate position looked shaky until brigades belonging to McLaws arrived in the nick of time to stem the tide. Rallying Wilcox's men, the rebels poured a withering storm of volley fire into the Federal troops, forcing them back to their original positions at the toll gate.

WILCOX SAVES THE DAY: THE BATTLE AT SALEM CHURCH

May 3-4, 1863 1045 - 1830 hours, viewed from the south-west. Sedgewick now attempted to link up with where he believed Hooker to be, unaware his superior had abandoned him to his fate. His delay in organising his troops allows Wilcox to fight a withdrawal from ridge to ridge back along the Telegraph Road. Instead of brushing Wilcox aside, Sedgewick fights him, but each minute Wilcox slows Sedgewick means Lee is a minute closer to supporting him.

Union troops manage to get as far as Salem Church as the Confederates continue to hit and run. Wilcox now errected breastworks across the road and awaits the attack knowing reinforcements in the form of McLaws and Anderson's brigades have now arrived. The time to stand and fight has now come.

Wilcox has chosen his ground, an area called the Toll Gate, about a mile east of Salem Church and the Union advances in the form of Brown's New Jersey brigade where heavy skirmishing takes place. Sedgewick slowly advances as the rebels fall back.

The tired New Yorkers attempting to take the road are met by the condensed fire of the now reinforced Confederate line and fall back towards the toll gate leaving nearly a third of their force behind.

That evening Howe arrived, and Sedgewick positioned his men north of the Turnpike to guard his rear and flanks, facing them south-east. The Confederates do not pursue their opportunity and that night the Union troops withdraw toward the northern Banks Ford before Confederate troops can coordinate and mount an offensive.

RIVER ROAD

TOLL GATE

TO FREDERICKSBURG

BROWN

UNION TROOPS	CONFEDERATE TROOPS
1 2nd New Jersey skirmishers	A Wofford
2 5th Maine	B Kershaw
3 96th Pennsylvania	C 8th Alabama
4 121st New York	D 10th Alabama
5 23rd New Jersey	E 9th Alabama
6 1st New Jersey	F 11th Alabama
7 3rd New Jersey	G 14th Alabama
8 95th Pennsylvania	H 10th Georgia
9 119th Pennsylvania	I 51st Georgia
10 16th New York	J 50th Gerogia
11 15th New Jersey	K 53rd Georgia
12 Newton	L Mahone
13 Howe	
14 Brooks	*For a full detailed unit*
15 Bartlett	*description see ORDER OF*
16 Brown	*BATTLE pages 27 - 35*

CHANCELLORSVILLE TODAY

Situated at what was a remote crossroads in 1863, today Chancellorsville battlefield spreads from the heart of downtown Fredericksburg to the bustling urban sprawl at Salem Church; the still rural-looking battlefield museum and entrenchments west of the city are two minutes from theaters, florists, and grocery stores, surrounded by sylvan housing projects. Ten minutes from downtown Fredericksburg, the battlefield museum lies six miles west off I-95 on State Road 3 (the east-west route of the Old Orange Turnpike), about ten miles west of the town of Fredericksburg and 45 miles south of Washington, D.C. The Plank Road is now paved, and is called State Road 610, running east-west a few miles south of SR 3. Here, history lies side by side with modern Virginia.

The Fredericksburg and Spotsylvania National Military Park is a collection of seven historically connected (but physically separated) sites which cover a total of nearly 8,000 acres. In the summer, re-enactors and park service officials dress up in period uniforms and costumes, and all year park rangers are available on

General F.T. Nicholls lost his left arm in the valley. Losing his foot at Fairview, he was knocked unconscious. Seeing the missing limbs, medics assumed he was dead, and left him on the battlefield. Later his men found him and revived him.

At Chancellorsville battlefield, just behind the visitor center, this stone monument to Jackson stands in a shady glade. Jackson was wounded a couple of hundred yards from here the night of 2 May 1863.

Salem Church was a two-story red brick church which rested on the south side of the Orange Turnpike. Here, Wilcox, aided by Kershaw and Wofford, stopped Sedgwick's advance.

Fitzhugh Lee, a nephew of General Lee, was one of J.E.B. Stuart's favorite cavalry commanders. After the war he brought a stone to the Chancellorsville battlefield as a commemoration of Stonewall Jackson for future generations of Americans.

a daily basis for information about the battlefield and the history behind it. A free map, which shows a route for a self-guided tour of all seven sites, is available at visitor centers. At Chatham the Stonewall Jackson Shrine is open daily during the summer and at certain times the rest of the year. All visitor centers are handicapped-accessible. An 11-mile hiking trail loops around the Spotsylvania site. There are no overnight camping facilities at the battlefield parks (which close at dusk) but 37 miles north (off I-95, a few miles before Washington, D.C.), the Prince William Forest Park offers a good place to camp.

Today the Chancellor house remains only as foundation ruins roped off with marker tapes. It was rediscovered and excavated in the mid-1970s, and it is marked by signs which briefly identify its significance. At the edge of the parking lot a tall, glass-protected four-color painting depicts the house in 1863, in flames, while Confederates point purposefully toward the woods to the north.

Scarcely two miles west of the Chancellor house lies the Chancellorsville museum and park, which closes at dusk. The National Park Service produces a good, free map and thumbnail history of Civil War battles in this area, entitled *Fredericksburg and Spotsylvania*. The museum's color slide-show puts not only Chancellorsville but its precursor, Fredericksburg, in perspective against the entire tapestry of Civil War history. The single-storey museum has enough uniforms, rifles, and personal memorabilia to bring the historical facts to life. There are tours of the immediate site roughly once an hour; these fill in smaller details of history, such as how Stoneman was an unusual choice for Hooker's cavalry commander because he suffered from piles!

The real attraction at the Chancellorsville museum, however, lies about 100 feet southwest of the visitor center, in a grove which seems quiet until automobiles zoom down SR 3, less than 20 feet away and destroy the reverie. A simple paved walkway leads to the grove surrounded by trees on the left and right, with a high hedge growing immediately behind it. In the middle of this 30-foot-wide grove Stonewall Jackson's monument rises to about 25 feet, a simple gray stone obelisk with an inscription or dedication on each of its four sides. On this spot Stonewall fell in the moonlight, wounded in the confusion by skirmishers from his own army.

Just 20 feet to the left of the obelisk grove lies an unpaved path, worn free of grass, where sits a large boulder in an obscure clearing. In 1876 Fitzhugh Lee initiated the idea of a lasting monument to Stonewall Jackson by bringing a light gray and white flecked boulder to this site. The nondescript boulder rests behind a modest placard with a photograph showing Fitzhugh Lee dressed in a dark suit

Taken at the Chancellorsville visitor center, this shows the area where Jackson fell. Even today the heavy woods would make visibility on a clear night difficult, and on a foggy night, visibility is drastically limited.

and waistcoat and standing next to this same chunk of stone in thick woods – these very woods as they were 120 years ago. For many years this boulder, pulled from Virginia's soil, was the only monument to Jackson, but today it is overshadowed by the more Napoleonic-looking obelisk. In this reverent glade, with traffic accelerating almost close enough to touch, the boulder alone does not appear to have changed. It does not take much imagination to picture this site with moonlight filtering fretfully through the trees, the crackle of musketry not too far away, and horses clopping softly on the red clay of a dirt road. This place does not raise the hairs on the back of your neck, but it does inspire visitors to converse in low, quiet tones.

Heading back toward Fredericksburg, Salem Church lies to the south side of SR 3 on a slight rise. A new church, erected in the late 1950s, occupies a spot just east of the original Salem Church. Between the historic church and the new house of worship lies the graveyard, which is separated from the actual church grounds by a split rail fence. Parking is in a gravel lot just south of the church grounds – it can take about ten automobiles. Cherry trees here flower in late April, and mockingbirds pick at the small ripening fruit where the wounded and dying were carried 135 years ago. A worn path, 150 yards long, leads to the church, screened by a smattering of trees.

Trees shield Salem Church from the sight of automobiles on the west, and people shopping at the mall north of the road can see the historic church on its little knoll across the highway. The square red brick building stands two stories high and has white framed windows on each wall. Its entrance faces south. It appears scenic and pastoral until one studies the brick walls carefully. Holes the size of a silver dollar pockmark the walls – bullet holes – mute evidence of the fierce fighting that took place here and of subsequent generations of souvenir hunters who dug bullets from the bricks with penknives.

The greater Fredericksburg-Chancellorsville area might be compared to Poland historically. This area is on a natural invasion route, and a dozen times Union and Confederate armies fought over portion of this ground. Much of

Viginia east of the Shenandoah Valley and Blue Ridge Mountains and south of Manassas and Culpepper was fought and re-fought in the early years of the war. Wilderness, Spotsylvania, Yellow Tavern, Brandy Station, Fredericksburg, Chancellorsville are well-known battlefields, yet to visit them today, one is struck by the simple pastoral beauty and the speedy repair work of Mother Nature who has covered the battlegrounds with secondary growth, filled in trenches and emplacements with erosion, creeper vines, and scrub oak, leaving those earthworks little more than depressions. As early as the 1890's much of the area was overgrown. It was not until recently that archeologists and historians again brought the foundations of the Chancellor House to light after the fire which destroyed it. Time and history are ever overshadowed by time and nature in this area.

Today Fredericksburg lies on the banks of a sluggish river. Where frames of burned and shell-shattered buildings stood in the winter of 1862 and spring of 1863 lie scores of small businesses. The visitor center in downtown Fredericksburg is almost surrounded by tourist businesses. Antique shops dot the areas where shells landed; coffee shops and used book stores cover the ground where Early opposed Sedgwick's advance before withdrawing. At Marye's Heights, the Fredericksburg Battlefield Museum sits below the crest of the hill near the stone wall and overlooks the riverbank.

The downtown Fredericksburg visitor center has an impressive multimedia show which gives not only the Civil War history of Fredericksburg, but also colonial and later history. A few trees shade the street, and hungry tourists can grab a snack or drink at more than a dozen eating places within a half-mile walk. It requires a good imagination to reflect upon the Civil War during a busy afternoon, but after dinner, when town is almost empty, a honeysuckle-scented spring breeze wafts slowly up from the river, hinting at a history that is really not all that distant.

WARGAMING CHANCELLORSVILLE 1863

Chancellorsville is an unusual battle whose separate phases occur miles apart. The battle can be broken into scenarios governing areas where actions took place:

1. Hooker's advance to Chancellorsville, including Sedgwick's southern diversion and Stoneman's raid; the Confederate withdrawing actions.

2. Early's position at Fredericksburg opposing Sedgwick's diversion.

3. Couch versus the Confederates at U.S. Ford.

4. Jackson's march where his rear elements were attacked; Jackson's march resulting in his surprise attack on XI Corps.

5. The Union's gradual withdrawal from Chancellorsville to form a new defensive line; action at Hazel Grove; action at Fairview; Hill and Stuart's assaults.

6. Sedgwick's breakthrough at Marye's Heights; Early's countermarch; Salem Church; Union retreat to Banks Ford.

Scenario 1 is very one-sided. The cavalry raid by Stoneman resulted in only a few burned bridges and had little effect on the outcome of the battle. As something to game, it should be dismissed. To game the Union advance on Chancellorsville, a strategic and sweeping approach is needed, and although there were some good skirmishes, such as the Union cavalry action versus the pickets at the river crossing, by and large this is not suitable for gamers who enjoy tactical actions. This scenario is grand strategy, best played on a board. The real game is not of conflict but of position and misdirection. The Union objective is to move units from several directions in order to occupy Chancellorsville as quickly as possible. The Confederate objective is to give ground slowly and form a defensive line.

Scenario 2 is a static game which offers little action, although many troops are shuffled around. A hidden movement situation and head to head conflict over just where and even *if* the Union intends an urban offensive is what is worthy of gaming here. The actual action could be an anti-climax to the situational mind game, as the Union player tries to find the Confederate weak point. Hidden movement is necessary because the Confederates are easily the weaker force and need to move troops behind their positions and keep the Union guessing as to their actual strength and disposition. The Union strategy is to probe for weak points and then to smash through, but in so doing, the Union has to probe several areas at once and will want to keep the Confederates off-guard as to which of the several probes will materialize into the actual assault area. The Confederate objective is to delay the Union as long as possible. The Union objective is to break through with as few casualties as possible to free the Orange Pike and link up with Chancellorsville.

Scenario 3 is actually a small sideline to Scenario 1, but it offers the greatest potential, for when the Union realized that some Confederate units were north

At Manassas battlefield park a large statue of an overcoated and mounted Stonewall Jackson faces north and overlooks the fields of First and Second Manassas.

of Fredericksburg and potentially able to swoop in on their flank, part of XI Corps was split off. The Southerners wisely withdrew before the superior Union units and re-formed astraddle the Orange Pike before the units could engage and lock in combat. This is a good withdrawing action, where the Southerners have to move quickly and decisively lest they find themselves cut off and overrun by elements of II Corps. The Union objective is to occupy as much ground as possible, while leaving no Confederate units as threats to its flanks or rear. The Confederate objective is to give ground slowly and fall back east-southeast toward Fredericksburg.

Scenario 4 is a good read, and what any gamer would love if he was playing the Confederates. It is difficult to game because in setting up the scenario, gamers have to be careful not to structure it so all the Union does is rout. If a gamer was playing the Union side, the challenge would not be *whether* his units routed, but how many, how fast, and how soon they could be rallied to make a stand. All units would not rout at the same time, nor at the same rate, thus making the Confederate advance irregular.

The Confederate player needs to smash as many Federals as possible to create as many demoralized and routing troops, while not outdistancing his command and control. The Union strategy is to fall back in as orderly a fashion as possible, thus having those units facing the approaching Southerners buy as much time for those units to their rear, so the rearward units could form a defensive line which would hold. If the Union player was aggressive and lucky, he could form troops and perhaps mount a counterattack; if the Confederate player was good, his goal would be to occupy Chancellorsville crossroads before midnight. The Union objective is to save troops. The Confederate objective is to rout Federals while taking as much ground as possible before nightfall. This game should be limited to five or six hours of game time, 25% of the game time in full daylight, 50% at dusk, and 25% in the dark. Points should be given for every scale one hundred yards of distance either player occupies or gives up between the Chancellorsville crossroads and the edge of the Spotsylvania Wilderness woods, where XI Corps was camped when Jackson attacked.

Scenario 5 offers a good stand-up fight, as the Confederates advance on Hazel Grove and Hooker decides to abandon it, while shelling them from Fairview. The Confederate advance on Fairview is more difficult. More importantly, the Union has lines of makeshift breastworks to fall back on during Stuart's assaults, and essentially the Confederates are in the position here that the Union commander is in with Scenario 1, because he cannot easily decide where the Union weak point is, so he cannot mass enough troops to attack and break through without direct frontal assaults and probes. The Union strategy here is to provide a holding action, giving ground as slowly as possible while forcing the Confederates to smash themselves against fortified positions. The Union objective is to conserve as many means possible while withdrawing and do it while inflicting as many casualties on the Southerners as possible. The Confederate objective is to take ground and bottle the Union Army up so it cannot find ways to cross the river and escape.

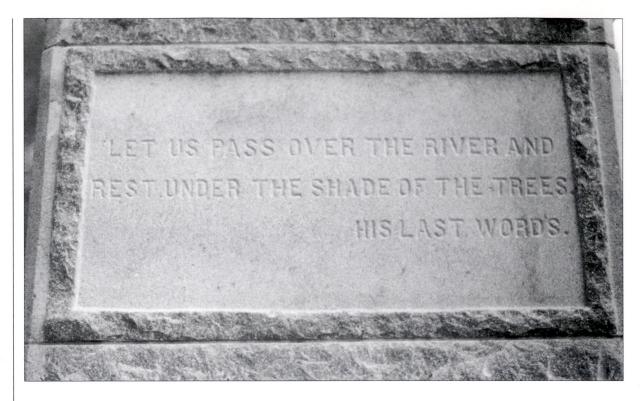

Scenario 6 is similar to the earlier Fredericksburg assault but in this scenario the Union conducts probing assaults and the Confederates have less hidden movement, which enables Union commanders to decide more effectively where to break the thin gray line. Once the Union breaks through, Early's men can return. However, do they make for Fredericksburg or Chancellorsville, or try to intercept the Federals en route to Chancellorsville? This part of Scenario 6 is really a strategic movement situation. The real battle occurs at Salem Church. The Federals come on strong. However, each turn brings new Confederate reinforcements, and the initial forward-thrusting mind set of the Union changes from one of uniting with Hooker's main body to preserving Sedgwick's command. Salem Church is a good stand-up fight. However, the real battle is not in the engagement, but in the disengagement and retreat toward Banks Ford. Even though the Confederates receive reinforcements, they should not have so many troops that they can pursue Sedgwick with impunity, because the Confederate troops will be wearied and they will have no reserves if they take a severe beating. Confederate command control is a real issue in this scenario because of McLaws' refusal to advance. The Union objective is to secure a river crossing north of Chancellorsville. The Confederate objective is to inflict as many Union casualties as possible.

Whatever the gamer's taste, Chancellorsville offers a variety of actions, from grand strategic to tactical. Although segmented, this allows gamers to experience the full feel of command if all segments are addressed; players cannot throw everything into the battle because they have to be aware of two fronts.

This plaque on the Stonewall Jackson monument commemorates his last words: "Let us pass over the river and rest under the shade of the trees." In his last moments, was he thinking of a Confederate offensive on the east bank of the Rappahannock?

INDEX

(References to illustrations are shown in **bold**. 'C.' = Chancellorsville.)